Cosmic Shift
A New Season of Faith

Christopher Paul Carter

For information contact The Fig and The Vine Publishing. Published by The Fig and The Vine Publishing, LLC

753 Winthrop St. Mt. Pleasant, SC 29466

thefigandthevinemedia.com

ISBN:
ISBN-10: 0988337061
ISBN-13: 978-0-9883370-6-0

Cover graphic design by:
Skye Como Miller, www.skyecomomiller.com

DEDICATION

To the adventurers, the travelers, the transitionaries:
I hope for you the words of an old Gaelic devotion,

"May you arrive at every place, may you return
home, may the way in which you spend be a way
without loss.

May every path before you be smooth, man,
woman, and child welcome you.

A truly good journey! Well does the fair Lord
show us a course, a path."

Contents

Preface

Dear Reader,

As I write this, winter is about to begin. In just a few weeks, we will experience the winter solstice, the shortest and darkest day of the year. Historically it's been a time of celebration, as almost every culture has a take on the feasting, dancing, and merrymaking that goes along with the beginning of brighter days. After the winter solstice the days get longer and longer. The sun shines more, and the earth creeps back into a new season of growth – and I love it. I love the sense of renewal and change. I don't necessarily like looking at trees with bare limbs, but I love how the emptiness is just a promise of new life to come. I completely understand why cultures all over the world, and throughout time, have made this moment a celebration to remember.

    I bring up the change in seasons to remind you of something. This change affects everyone. There is simply no escaping winter, although some folks have the financial means to hop a plane to a tropical climate and forget that the earth gets cold and dark. But the change is still affecting them, after all... it's making them move. So whether you enjoy it or avoid it, there is just no denying it affects you. No matter what hemisphere you live on, or in what climate, the earth goes through periodic changes. Even if the effects aren't felt in the form of temperature, it can still be sensed in the sky. The path of the sun is different. There are different stars in the night sky. These changes in time are part of existence for everyone on this earth.

This book is about a similar change in time. It's a change that, like winter, is both unavoidable and captivating. I've been feeling this change, deep down in my bones for some time. I know I'm not alone either, because everywhere I speak there is always a contingent of people who seem to come alive when we talk about the change. It's the changing of an age of man. This isn't a new topic, as you know. A "new age" has been in our modern vernacular for some time, close to a century now. This is as good a time as any to address the term "new age." Because it has fallen into some misuse and confusion, I've chosen to use another term altogether. I'm calling it the "next age." As I hope to explain in the coming pages, I think that is a better term anyway, because this is not the first time the earth has passed through one of these historic changes in time. It's just the "next" time.

Also, I believe this next age can't possibly be grasped without understanding God's history with man and the story of redemption. Conversely, the story of our redemption from sin and the fall can't be completely understood without a concept of how the ages change and the promise of a soon coming "new age." But I wouldn't be writing this book if I thought we knew all there was to know about a shift in the age. Furthermore, I wouldn't be writing this book at all if I didn't think there was a huge gap in our connection of the story of our redemption and this "new age."

For many Christians, this subject is to be avoided; and that's unfortunate. As I said before, it's like winter. You can stick your head in the ground and hope it blows by, but that is hardly going to keep you out of the cold. The age will change, and that change will affect the earth in the most profound ways. My hope is that by explaining the change, it will be less intimidating. Without the misunderstanding and fear, we can be excited about the next age and should we decide to, even participate in its arrival. It's the "participation" that's the big issue for me. I don't feel led to only observe the change, although that would still be a great step in the right direction. I feel a desire to move towards the next age with my actions, beliefs, and practices. As we will see, there is a historical precedent for that. The ages change only with human involvement, as if people all over the world are pulling open a massive cosmic door into a new chapter of our story – of God's story.

That's what the ages are all about. They're like chapters in a story. In our case, the story we've been reading for the last 6,000 years or so (you might know it as all of recorded human history), is the story of our fall from perfection and our Creator's plan to restore us. If I were going to give the story a title, I'd call it *The Redemption of Man*. In the pages to come, I'll show you just how close I believe we are to its completion. It's a staggering thought if you give it the time. The only story that mankind has been reading since, well... since ever, is nearly done. We are literally in its last chapter (if not its last paragraph). That should beg the question of all of us: What story will we read next, and what will it be called?

There's a certain feeling you get when you're reading the last pages of a good book. It's a sense of completion. There's also a warmth inside when you remember the good parts – the highlights. Then, there's the moment you realize something must come next, after you've finished. Maybe it's a sequel to the book, or perhaps a new story altogether, but it never occurs to us to stop reading and never pick up a book again. Of course we will pick out another book and keep on reading... there are still more stories to experience. So for everyone who wants to "keep reading" and see what's in the next story, this book is offered as a helpful guide. For to read the next story is to start to act it out; and that is a wild proposition.

I could think of no better title than *Cosmic Shift* because it summed up everything I wanted to cover: There is a new age dawning; the shift will change everything, just like it has in the past; it will bring with it a whole new story of God and man; and, even in the transition, humanity will be commissioned anew. Like any major reordering, it will have its unstable, bumpy moments. And the transition itself might be a particularly contested time. However, most changes in time, no matter how dark and cold they seem, merit a celebration, especially when that change marks the beginning of a new season of light.

As always, God speed on your journey,

Christopher

Part 1
The Ages

"As if you could kill time without injuring eternity"

- Henry David Thoreau

"Eternity is in love with the productions of time."

- William Blake

"For everything there is a season, and a time for every matter under Heaven..."

- Ecclesiastes 3:1

Chapter 1

It's About Time

Reconnecting with time will be our first step. Believe it or not, most of us in the modern world are missing the meaning of time. I don't mean that it's not important to us, because just about everyone is extremely time-focused. We order our day, plan our month, and schedule entire years in advance all on a system of time. Then, we check the time constantly. We look at clocks, we remind ourselves about appointments. We make sure we're not late and worry if we are. If there is one thing that tirelessly orders our day, it's time. But simply being aware or fixated on something doesn't mean we *understand* it. Or I could say that just because something is important, does not imply that we fully grasp it's meaning.

Take, for instance, the modern fixation on sex in the western world. Using America as an example, we can see the daily, constant barrage of sexual imagery and conversation. One could argue that, in America, sex is very important. However, the misuse, degradation, and commonness of it seems to imply (or at least it seems obvious to me) that we don't understand its meaning. When something is simultaneously very important and yet has lost its meaning, we get into some trouble. Either example (meaning time or sex) is important for all the right reasons – and that need not change. However, when the meaning is taken away or lost, the experience of either is distorted, and then we do have a case for a change. In the area of time, I think the distortion has harmed us far more than we know. Our importance/meaning imbalance in this field, has put us out of sync with one of the first conditions, or functions, of human life. But in order to see this, I need you to do a little thought exercise.

Imagine for a moment that you are standing out in a field. There are no trees around, so you have an unobstructed view of the horizon in every direction. Then imagine the sky above you is cloud free and crystal-clear blue. Now pretend you don't have to do anything for the next year except stand in that one spot (we're pretending you can do that without sleeping or getting tired, too) and watch the sky. What you would see over the days, weeks, and months, is one beautifully ordered and repetitive display. Bright orbs like the Sun and Moon, followed by lesser lights like the planets and twinkling stars, are all parts of the heavenly parade. If you could just watch it, and only do that for a year, you would be mystified by the periodic dance of lights all around you. It's ordered. It's colorful (stars have different colors if you've never noticed). And *it's one giant clock.*

The sky above our heads, and the lights that move in its medium, make up the first clock that mankind ever knew. I think that's obvious to us, even though we take it for granted these days. Long before digital clocks adorned the microwave and bedside table, and before circular dials were hung on the wall, there was the clock in the sky. I would argue that the heavenly clock is far more beautiful and effective than the modern imitations, and we'll get to that in a moment. First, I want to highlight something about the origin of that first clock, and what that can tell us about the meaning of time. To see it, let's read the account of the 4th day of creation in Genesis, Chapter 1:

> *Then God said, "Let there be lights in the firmament of the Heavens to divide the day from the night; and let them be for signs and seasons, and for days and years; and let them be for lights in the firmament of the Heavens to give light on the earth"; and it was so. Then God made two great lights: the greater light to rule the day, and the lesser light to rule the night. He made the stars also. God set them in the firmament of the Heavens to give light on the earth, and to rule over the day and over the night, and to divide the light from the darkness. And God saw that it was good. (Genesis 1: 14 – 18)*

"That makes the lights in the sky a really good clock and compass, if one should learn to read them."

Let's not breeze by the fact this clock was ordained by the Creator. He said it was a good thing, not a product of the fall of mankind. That's right, the use of the sun, moon, and stars for time keeping and guidance (He said they were for "signs" as well) was around before Adam and Eve fell from perfection. Today we Christians often rebuke the consultation of this (sky) clock – for any purpose – as an unholy act. That's natural considering how astrology has skewed the practice of seeking the meaning of the stars. Just remember, no matter what is being done in error in that respect, the heavenly lights were created for *precisely* this purpose. We'll see in a moment just how often astronomical signs are used in the Bible, but for now let's look at one prominent example.

The "wise men from the east" who came to give gifts to Jesus did so because of astronomical signs. They said that they followed His star, which means the cosmic clock not only told them it was time to seek the boy Jesus, but also pointed the way. That makes the lights in the sky a really good clock and compass, if one should learn to read them. While I cannot overstate the importance of reconnecting with this clock, it still doesn't tell the whole story about time. To see the origin of the idea of time, look a few verses back in Genesis, on the very first day of creation:

Then God said, "Let there be light"; and there was light. And God saw the light, that it was good; and God divided the light from the darkness. God called the light Day, and the darkness He called Night. So the evening and the morning were the first day. (Genesis 1:3 – 5)

Notice that we have evening, morning, and day and night *before* there was the sun and moon. It seems impossible to have a discussion about these verses and avoid the common argument about a literal interpretation versus a scientific approach and whether or not this is a chronological account of creation and on and on and on. I'm not going down that road, because sometimes I think we just need to read the words, themselves. Without trying to create a doctrinal deadlock with these statements, what could we get by just hearing them (or paying attention to them)? I think we can see that the idea or function of time existed before there were even lights to mark it. Or we might say that the function of time was more foundational because it was created first.

With that in mind, notice that this is a day 1 issue. And there isn't a lot else going on that day. It would seem a major focus of this first day is (even with its contrast of light and dark) to introduce the aspect of time. How important should this issue be to us? If it is the purpose of the first day, does that say something about how dependent the rest of creation was upon this foundation? I think so. I think time is made on day 1 because it is the framework for the rest of life. There was just no moving forward in creation without a sense of timing. Going one more step back in Genesis, and still deeper into time's meaning, we now look at the first words of the Bible:

In the beginning God created the Heavens and the earth.
(Genesis 1:1)

The first three words of the scriptures are a statement of time – "in the beginning". It could have started with anything. I think the phrase "Listen to this, humans!" would have been much more appropriate, given our propensity to do the opposite. But to the Creator, the most fitting words to begin the story, were to put that story into context. Now before you say, "Of course the first words of the Bible were 'in the beginning,' it's the start of the story after all!" just consider how it is that you understand the idea of a "start." Could you grasp a beginning, middle, climax, or ending (all parts of a good story arc) without a concept of time? If we took away this crucial and foundational sense of existence, then the events of this present moment, or your history, or your future, would lose their relation to each other; and it is precisely that relationship between events that gives them their meaning. Would the cross mean anything if it was not preceded by 4,000 years of frustration, death, and need?

"... to miss the context of the story is to miss the story altogether. I believe we are dangerously close to doing just that."

Again, it is our sense of *time* that provides us with an understanding of a story. We get that a story has to start somewhere. It has to build up momentum and establish a direction. It then needs to reach a point of no return, a climax of sorts, before it marches on to its conclusion. If you can think of time as the "arc" of the story, almost like the framework the story is built upon, then you will be a long way towards understanding its meaning. Conversely, to lose a sense of time is to lose the context. In that state the story arc degenerates, and you wouldn't know where you are in the story or what might be coming next. Even worse, you might stop progressing in the story at all – as if the loss of time pressed a pause button. The story will go on, but you might miss out on participating in it. Simply put, to miss the *context* of the story is to miss the story altogether. I believe we are dangerously close to doing just that.

Chapter 2

Imitating Time

Because this book is dealing with changes and meaning in time – on the grandest of scales – we have to reconnect with time as it was designed. We need to sense it again, which is something we don't do today; even though we are constantly observing it. Let's talk for a minute about how our modern world tells the time. Take, for example, the classic watch with the white dial and black numerals. The hands move about the dial uniformly, and each division of time is exactly the same as the one before it. It's a little boring to be honest. The hands of the watch march on against a backdrop that knows no changes. It's as if each little white space between the numbers is a homogenized volume of time. The space between the "1" and the "2" no different than the space between the "4" and "5."

Clocks are designed that way for a reason. The time between the numbers is, mathematically, the same. It takes 60 seconds – and only 60 seconds – to get from one minute division to the next. We know this of course, and we appreciate a watch's mathematical precision. But we lose something of the nature of time when it becomes homogenized. We lose its character. We lose its essence. None of these things can accurately be displayed on a watch because they are qualities, not quantities.

If we take it a step further, we can see how all our measures of time have followed suit. Our desk calendars give us the same uniform, white squares. Each day a clone of the one before it. Each month the same sized page with nearly the same number of squares to fill up with appointments. It would seem our modern view of time is like a cookie cutter, and we just observe each little same shaped piece of dough as it passes. And in its final evolution, our homogenized time takes the form of digital numbers on a backlit background, like what you see on your alarm clock or car dashboard. Our road to quantified time ended when we took even the motion out of it. For before, we could at least see the hands of the clock turn, implying some kind of change and progression. Now, in the digital age, time is just uniformly progressing numbers.

However, deep down we do sense time differently than our industrialized clocks would have us believe. For example, we all feel a change in our moods and outlooks when a favorite season arrives. It's hard to put into numbers just how we feel about a season. Furthermore, even though we experience it every year, none of us would say we lived the same season twice. Each one is different; each one has its own story with distinctive qualities. Each progression in time, with its particular flavor of events, means something a little different to us. It's this sense of progression and meaning that we've lost, even though it's always felt in the back of our minds, when we settle for a quantified – and only a quantified – view of time.

"... you could look at the sky non stop for your entire life and never see the same "clock" twice."

The clinically uniform time we've become accustomed to disappears when we take a look at the cosmic clock that God made for us. That clock has a sun, moon, and planets (again, all with varying colors) moving against a backdrop of stars. The moon is always going through different phases. The sun is rising and setting at different points on the eastern and western horizons. The planets are marching a path through the stars at totally different rates. Far from homogenized, this clock is ever changing. In fact, you could look at the sky non stop for your entire life and never see the same "clock" twice.

It's as if the earth is a raft floating down a river of time, and the current is constantly changing. Even in the exact same spot on the river, the current won't be exactly the same. And all around the earth, as it follows the flow of time, the scenery is constantly changing. Something new around every bend. You can see how this view of time – as a current we are moving through (recall again our comparison to a story arc) – is lost in our modern observations. Can you imagine how different mankind's development would have been if, instead of a beautiful time-keeping firmament above our heads, all we saw was a giant backlit display with faded green numbers ticking off a 24 hour schedule? Time, in this hypothetical world, would just be a cold, feelingless calculation.

Thankfully, that is not our history, and all of those beautiful stars up there have been an occupation of mankind for a long, long time. From the beginning, we knew to watch them. We knew, just like the magi, that the firmament told a constantly evolving story. In just a moment, we are going to see how the stars, grouped together as constellations, could tell us something through their names and signs. The constellations, after all, make pictures. And those pictures have been with mankind since we could pass things down via oral tradition.

Let us be reminded again that the terms – pictures… story – evoke a sense of meaning that a digital clock simply can't replicate. What would mean more to you, that it is noon on September 5th – or that the light that rules the day is smack dab in the middle of a picture of a lion? For that is what noon on September 5th really is. That is a day when the sun is in the constellation Leo. Leo is a lion, and that picture is rich with meaning. When the brightest light in the firmament is residing directly overhead in the "sign" of the lion, I would think the sky is trying to tell us something.

"It is nearly impossible for most Americans to even see the cosmic clock anymore. Where did it go? It has vanished from our view!"

All of this is to say that if every step away from the clock our Creator gave us is numbing us to a fundamental aspect of life, shouldn't we get reacquainted with time as it was meant to be? Unfortunately, there is much standing in the way of that pursuit. For starters, no one looks at the sky anymore. I have found this to be categorically true for people in a modern, western society. We simply never think to look up and become familiar with the firmament. If we did a quick inventory of our time, I think we would see why we don't bother.

We are inside for most of our lives, particularly at night. There are many modern inventions and conveniences that keep us inside. For instance, having a controlled climate inside means less time outside in the summer. In the winter, we can stay inside and read by lamplight when the days grow dark. Also, all the things that we "look" at these days are inside. If you're going to spend time gazing at something, isn't it normally a screen? The internet, television, and video games are all activities that fill up our quota for "looking." When that need is met, the drive to observe anything is diminished.

If we start looking for the point in history when we ceased observing the firmament, we might hone in on the 2nd industrial revolution, also sometimes called the technological revolution. From the late 1800's to the early 1900's there were many developments that shaped modern life. One of these was electricity. Once there was a ready source of power inside the home, all sorts of time consuming technologies appeared, starting perhaps with the radio. All of this is a relatively recent change. 100 years or so of electric power is a blink of the eye, historically speaking. It may seem odd to us that just a few generations ago, people were still familiar with the cosmic clock.

Since this is such a recent development, you would think the journey back to the cosmic clock wouldn't be that hard. Think again. It is nearly impossible for most Americans to even see the cosmic clock anymore. Where did it go? It has vanished from our view! With the advent of electricity, artificial lights sprang up everywhere. There are now so many street lights, building lights, and home lights that the natural lights are overpowered. And this is what makes it all seem so devious to me: We are distracted to the point of losing our interest and knowledge of the night sky, and then we are prohibited from reconnecting with it – if we ever broke free from the distractions – by the very system that created the distractions. To someone who desperately wants to find meaning again in time, this seems like a cruel trap. When we stopped looking at the sky, our new pastimes went to work erasing our connection to time itself by replacing the natural lights with imitations. It kinda seems like it was done on purpose...

To see just how much has been erased, consider that during a major electricity blackout in Los Angeles, in 1994, people called 911 concerned about the "strange clouds" overhead. Turns out, it was the rich star fields of the Milky Way, which most had never seen before due to the artificial lights. Personally, the only truly dark sky I have ever stood under was in Arizona while visiting the Grand Canyon. Where I live, east of the Mississippi River, there are virtually no dark skies. That means that it is impossible to see the sky as God created it in these developed areas. But that was not the case in Arizona, and I couldn't stop staring at the stars. I spent hours just looking at the cloudy, white ribbon of the Milky Way stretching from one end of the sky to the other. To anyone who has not seen it, you need to put this on your bucket list. Find a dark sky and see the firmament – and time – as you were meant to.

If we can bear to hear it, our current view of time is recent and unnatural. Remember that we are the first people in the history of mankind to *not see the cosmic clock*, and to many of us that might not even seem like a big deal. I hope this chapter goes a long way to convince us all that time and the firmament, inextricably linked together, make up one of the fundamental building blocks of existence. To deny it, or to simply not care that it is passing away, is to weaken the foundation of life. I invite you to consider your history, both recent and ancient, as we look at one of the oldest (if not the oldest) books of the Bible. In it, we can find a very early record of how mankind viewed time and the cosmic clock:

> *Canst thou bind the sweet influences of Pleiades, or loose the bands of Orion? Canst thou bring forth Mazzaroth in his season? or canst thou guide Arcturus with his sons? Knowest thou the ordinances of Heaven? Canst thou set the dominion thereof in the earth? (Job 38: 31 – 33 KJV)*

Have you ever felt the sweet influences of the constellation known as the Pleiades? Have you ever felt the dominion of the stars over the earth? These words hearken back to a time when the firmament was felt and sensed far more than it was calculated. We get the picture again of a current or flow of time that can have as noticeable an effect on us as a change in the weather. By definition, an "influence" is something that affects your character or behavior. Is it so strange to think of time as something that influences us? Can you imagine it like a cosmic river whose changes and movements affect you on the deepest level? Your ancestors certainly did. Using the industrial revolution again as a marker, consider that 97% of human history was founded on the cosmic clock, leaving only 3% with our modern imitations. Surely, there must be something we can reclaim from 5,800 years of actually seeing time.

Chapter 3

The Mazzaroth

There are some obvious regularities in the celestial clock: The rising of the sun and moon for instance; and on a yearly scale, the seasonal progression of the constellations. Predictably, each spring we can see Leo high in the night sky, and each winter Orion makes its debut. Another regularity is visible if we track the path of the sun (disclaimer: never look at the sun, you'll go blind). Month by month, we would see the sun moving against the backdrop of stars. It's an effect of the earth's orbit around the sun, and there are plenty of good teaching visuals on youtube if you need to see how the geometry works. This yearly path through the stars forms the "frame" of the cosmic clock, as it takes the sun through 12 constellations, which many of us know today as the zodiac constellations. However, there is a much older name for these star-pictures, and we just read it in the passage from the book of Job:

Can you bring out Mazzaroth in its season?

"Mazzaroth" is the old Hebrew name for these 12 focal constellations, and we can think of it as the backdrop – or frame – of the cosmic clock. Furthermore, all of the 12 signs are rich with obvious meaning. I want to familiarize you with these pictures, and I think the simplest approach is to ask, "What does this picture say about the Father or His plan? What does this sign say about our journey from the fall of man back to perfection?" I'll give you the name of the constellation, what it depicts, and then make some comments about its meaning. This is not exhaustive, just an overview.

Libra: *A set of measures or scales. This depicts God's justice, assessment, and balance, along with the Law of Moses.*

Virgo: *A virgin woman, holding a sheaf of wheat. This is a picture of the harvest, a bride, Israel, and the mother of Jesus.*

Leo: *A lion. Lions are a picture of kingship. We could think of ruling, authority, or declarations.*

Cancer: *A crab, although in some old Mazzaroth images, it has been a turtle, crayfish, or lobster. In any case, these are lowly creatures. They inhabit the floor of the ocean, which is even below the land, and none of these creatures stand tall. It is a picture of humility and service, which explains why the brightest stars in this constellation are named the Northern and Southern Donkey. Donkeys are another obvious display of servitude. Also, Cancer is the dimmest constellation in the zodiac. A humble sign on every level.*

Gemini: *The twins. Two people who are a mirror image of each other might make us think of the creation of man. When God made man, He made him in His image. The word "image" means reflection. So it can be said that God made man in His reflection.*

This perfect symmetry between two people could also depict a covenant, like marriage. Also, it points to Adam and Eve, the first two people created.

Taurus: *The bull. Strength and power were all historical attributes of a bull or ox, and are defining characteristics of the Lord. This is also an aggressive, militant sign.*

Aries: *The ram (or in some Mazzaroths, a lamb). A picture of sacrifice, purity, and the crucifixion.*

Pisces: *Two fish bound together and being hauled out of the water. Pulling fish out of the water is an image of provision, but there is another element of things being joined together. Think of the joining of Jew and Gentile into one new man as an example. Also, as much emphasis as Jesus put on being a "fisher of men," I would think this also speaks of rescuing humanity out of the waters of destruction.*

Aquarius: *A man pouring out water from a vessel, also called the water bearer. The water itself should remind us of the Holy Spirit, who has been called a river of living water. Sometimes the man is portrayed with wings, which portrays a heavenly, immortal, and perfected man.*

Capricorn: *The goat horn. Contrary to the modern take on this sign, it is more about the horn of the goat than it is the goat. The horn can be a symbol of a shofar or be related to our concept of a cornucopia, also known as a horn of plenty. In the case of the shofar, we could imagine God sending out a message. At times in the*

Bible, angels are seen blowing these instruments. As for the horn of plenty, our God certainly values abundance and prosperity.

Sagittarius: *The archer. Forget the half man/half horse picture. This word simply means "archer." Two pictures come to mind from the scriptures. The first deals with the Law, called the Torah. The word "Torah," comes from a root that means "to hit the mark." This is properly translated as "instruction" or "teaching." However, the root word conjures up a Sagittarius hitting the bullseye. Another significant "archer and arrow" theme comes from the description in Psalm 127 of sons being like arrows in the quiver. We could take that picture even further and consider this sign an image of romantic and procreative love. In fact, it may relate to our idea of Cupid shooting his arrows.*

Scorpio: *The scorpion. Also, by association with the constellation directly above it in the sky, the serpent. This is the only negative sign in the Mazzaroth. It is the sign of death and mortality, and it's where we get the idea of the "sting of death." It is related to the serpent, which is eternally connected to our idea of satan. This is not the final word on this constellation though; keep reading to see how the Creator redeemed this sign in the cosmic clock.*

See Figure 1 page 33

I will encourage you to consider how these signs influence life on earth each month. You might think of it this way: When the sun is in a particular sign, it is illuminating, or highlighting, that sign. It's not as if that image and its characteristics are the only thing the Father is thinking about; rather, during that time, it is a celebration of that attribute. When the sun is in Leo, time itself is celebrating His (and our) kingship over creation, along with His authority and declarations. When the sun is in Sagittarius, there is a celebration of romantic love and so on. Considering these signs each month will be the beginning of our reconnection with the currents that were felt way back in the time of Job. Sadly, there aren't many reliable sources to which we can turn to tell us what time is celebrating in a particular month. Observation is about the only fool proof method. As stated before, that is unlikely to happen simply because of artificial lights. So in the meantime, check out one of the many applications available for computers and smart phones that help you with this. It's unfortunate, but the same technology responsible for blocking out the lights is about our only reasonable option. It is, however, better than nothing.

While we could go on about the benefits of getting in the flow of time, this book has to keep marching forward towards a discussion of the next age, which means we have to finish our discussion of the Mazzaroth. To see how central these 12 cosmic signs were to God, let's consider how He overtly implanted them into the beginnings of the nation, Israel. If you are familiar with the history of Israel, you know there were some patriarchs, starting with Abraham. Abraham fathered Isaac, who in turn fathered Jacob. It was Jacob who had 12 sons, the number of which is our first clue that God's cosmic plan is about to make an appearance. On his deathbed Jacob gives his sons their blessings (Genesis 49), and it's in these blessings the signs of the Mazzaroth begin to emerge. In this case, it is seen in the 3 sons listed below.

Judah *is called a lion.*

Reuben *is related to water.*

Dan *is called a serpent.*

The 12 sons became the foundations of the 12 tribes of Israel. It is these same 12 tribes that Moses led out of Egypt; and upon his death, he also pronounced a blessing on each tribe *(Deuteronomy 33)*. Of particular interest to us is the blessing he gives Joseph (which was passed on to Ephraim).

Joseph *is compared to the horns of the bull or ox.*

By itself these blessings wouldn't seem to point to the cosmic clock at all, except by happenstance. However, let's take into account a few more scriptures. When the Israelites left Egypt, Moses received instructions on how to set up the tabernacle, along with directions on how to place the tribes, with their thousands upon thousands of people (Numbers, chapter 2). Each tribe was to encamp under the banners of 4 ruling tribes. These 4 tribes were placed at the cardinal points around the tabernacle, on the North, South, East, and West. Not surprisingly, the 4 tribes picked for this job were Judah, Ephraim, Reuben, and Dan.

See Figure 2

FIGURE 1

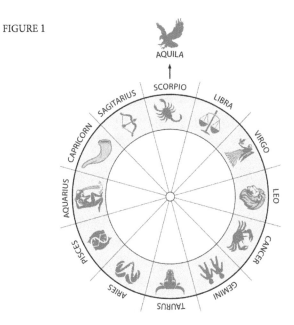

FIGURE 2

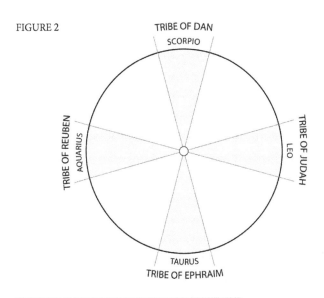

FIGURE 1: The Signs of the Mazzorath
FIGURE 2: The Ruling Tribes and Cardinal Signs of the Mazzorath

"To us, the connection between the Mazzaroth and the foundation of Israel may seem like a hidden secret, buried deep in the scriptures for only the astronomically savvy to find. I disagree. There is nothing subtle about millions of people encamped under these 4 signs, surrounding a tabernacle filled with God's bright presence."

If you're putting the pieces of the puzzle together, then you can imagine a central tabernacle of worship (with a glowing column of cloud and fire above it), surrounded by 4 banners: Lion, Bull, Water-bearer, and Serpent. It's starting to look a lot like the 4 cardinal points of the Mazzaroth. Perhaps the best instance of someone noticing this pattern comes from the story of Balaam. You can read the whole story from Numbers, chapter 22 through 24. I'll give you the paraphrase here.

Balaam, a sorcerer of sorts, is hired by the King of Moab to curse the Israelites. The Israelites were encamped around the tabernacle according to the order I mentioned above, and we can see Balaam discover the cosmic plan for their organization one step at a time as he attempts to curse Israel. He makes his first statement from a spot near the camp when he makes some comments about the shear number of Israelites followed by a blessing instead of a curse. Predictably, the king of Moab is upset and brings Balaam to a higher place for his cursing in the hopes of getting his money's worth. From the "top of Pisgah," where Balaam could see "the outer part" of the camp, he ends up releasing another blessing. But from this height he can see a little more of the encampment, and says Israel "has strength like a wild ox" and "is like a lion." It's important to note here that Balaam is a diviner, also likely an astrologer, and certainly had knowledge of the constellations. Could he have been seeing the order of the cosmos?

Again, the king of Moab is infuriated and demands Balaam try again. So he takes the diviner up to an even higher place, "to the top of Peor, that overlooks the wasteland." Now Balaam is so high that "he saw Israel encamped according to their tribes." It must have been high up, indeed, for the sorcerer to see this massive throng of people, and to distinguish one tribe from another. Also, how is it that he could determine one tribe from another, unless there were some clear separations and markers, like the banners we mentioned earlier? But we don't have to guess at what Balaam was seeing. In this 3rd prophetic blessing, he finally sees the cosmic order of the camp of Israel:

> *How lovely are your tents, O Jacob!*
> *Your dwellings, O Israel!*
> *He shall pour water from his buckets,*
> *And his seed shall be in many waters...*
>
> *God brings him out of Egypt;*
> *He has strength like a wild ox...*
>
> *He bows down, he lies down as a lion;*
> *And as a lion, who shall rouse him? (Numbers 24:5 – 9)*

From the top of Peor, Balaam looked out over the camp of Israel and saw the central tabernacle surrounded by the 4 cardinal signs of the Mazzaroth. He acknowledges, in order, the Aquarius (water-bearer), Taurus, and Leo. Anyone would have to admit that the phrase "He shall pour water from his buckets," is an odd phrase unless it is a reference to the constellation, Aquarius.

To us, the connection between the Mazzaroth and the foundation of Israel may seem like a hidden secret, buried deep in the scriptures for only the astronomically savvy to find. I disagree. There is nothing subtle about millions of people encamped under these 4 signs, surrounding a tabernacle filled with God's bright presence. To any observer (and especially to Balaam) this would have looked like the order of the Heavens come down to earth. It was, in every respect, the structure of the cosmos reflected in the people of Israel. By the way, if you're wondering why the sorcerer doesn't mention the 4th banner/sign that divided the camp in his 3rd prophecy, it's because of a play on words. The word for "serpent" in Hebrew is the same word for "sorcerer." You can imagine Balaam standing on the high mountain and seeing the banners of the Mazzaroth to his right, left, and center, and then realizing that he is standing in the place of the serpent/sorcerer. I bet Balaam was stunned.

Still, there are even more times the structure of the Mazzaroth pops up in the scriptures. Take a look at the description of the cherubim, also called living creatures, from the book of Ezekiel. This is also the part where we see how God redeems the sign of the scorpion-serpent.

Then I looked, and behold, a whirlwind was coming out of the north, a great cloud with raging fire engulfing itself; and brightness was all around it and radiating out of its midst like the color of amber, out of the midst of the fire. Also from within it came the likeness of four living creatures. And this was their appearance: they had the likeness of a man. Each one had four faces;

As for the likeness of their faces, each had the face of a man; each of the four had the face of a lion on the right side, each of the four had the face of an ox on the left side, and each of the four had the face of an eagle. (Ezekiel 1: 4 – 10)

These angelic beings are also spotted by John as he penned the book of Revelation:

And in the midst of the throne, and around the throne, were four living creatures full of eyes in front and in back. The first living creature was like a lion, the second living creature like a calf, the third living creature had a face like a man, and the fourth living creature was like a flying eagle.

Surrounding the throne in Heaven are 4 signs, just like the ones surrounding Israel's tabernacle – with one prominent exception. Instead of a scorpion or serpent, we have an eagle, which leaves us with a whole different feeling or sense of meaning about that sign. An eagle would symbolize something heavenly or revelatory. Also, the strength of the eagle is its sight, so this sign should make us think of perception, or even prophecy. If you're asking if it's all right for God to just replace the only negative – or lost – sign of the Mazzaroth with something positive, just consider another group of 12 we are all familiar with. Jesus had 12 disciples after all, and of those 12, how many went bad and had to be replaced? Just one. And it was critical to the disciples that Judas' place was restored. The restoration of a fallen position is part of the plan that we see in the Heavens. Therefore, when we see the angelic living creatures, we are seeing the order of the Heavens restored.

Even the gospels, themselves, have been compared to the 4 cardinal signs of the Mazzaroth. The gospels of Matthew, Mark, and Luke can be seen accentuating the human, kingly, and powerful nature of Jesus. Finally, John's gospel is decidedly eagle-like in its heavenly, divine view of Jesus. There is a wonderful 8th century illustration from the Book of Kells that depicts this very comparison (see Figure 3). The bottom line here is that the structure of the firmament, and of time, was fashioned into the foundation of the tribes, the prophets, the gospels, and even the last book of the Bible. We shouldn't be surprised by this: It was God's invention and He didn't hide it out of sight, even though our current blindness would have us believe otherwise.

FIGURE 3

FIGURE 3: The Four Gospels from "The Book of Kells"

Chapter 4

From Age to Age

There's one more aspect of the cosmic clock we need to discuss before we can move on, and it's the feature that best shows how the firmament, and time, are telling our story. To see it, you need to know about the spring equinox. It's the moment of the year when the earth has an equal number of daylight and nighttime hours. The word "equinox" is a Latin word meaning "equal night." Equinoxes and their opposites, the solstices, are important times of the year for different reasons. As stated earlier, the winter solstice was important because it was the promise of a new season of light and longer days. The vernal (spring) equinox is a fixture in life because it marks the beginning of the year. Notice that the Hebrew calendar has its first month during this time. It is a natural choice. Springtime is a season of new beginnings and new growth.

As you can imagine, early observers gave special attention to the Mazzaroth signs during these moments, and that of course meant knowing the sign in which the sun was residing. You'd expect that every year the sun would be in the same position, and in the same sign, at the spring equinox, but that is not the case. The path of the sun has a very slow progression backwards through the signs of the Mazzaroth. And when I say "slow" I mean really, really slow. The sun moves about 1 degree of a 360 degree circle every 70 years or so. That means it was just barely perceptible over the span of one human life. To an early star watcher, this was an important shift, and it was possible to figure out how long it would take the sun to move from one sign to the next. Again, using the spring equinox as the guidepost, they knew it would take about 2,100 years for the equinox to shift one whole sign. Also, since there are 12 signs, it would take about 26,000 years for the spring equinox to move through the entire Mazzaroth!

*Some quick notes: Basically, the movement of the equinoxes is caused by a wobble in the earth's rotation about its axis (think of a top wobbling as it spins on a table). I would advise you to take the time to learn about why this happens on your own. It's far easier to learn the geometry of the precession of the equinoxes visually, so some videos on Youtube.com will go a long way.

"The disciples were not scholars or astronomers, yet they had in their everyday vocabulary a word for the 2,100 year progression of time. It shouldn't be lost on us that an "age" was a well known concept..."

This 26,000 year cycle was a known quantity to early cultures, which makes sense when you consider that they observed and studied the firmament in ways that are lost on us today. It was easy for them to see the sun moving through the signs; and the information would have been passed down the generations, from one astronomer to the next, until the pattern was understood. This pattern was the longest periodic cycle they had seen, which gave it special significance. To some early cultures, this 26,000 year motion was called the "great year." The 2,100 year periods marked by the Spring Equinox were called "months of the great year." They were also called "ages." When you stop and think about it, this term is often used as a historical reference and in music. I think everyone has heard the song "Age of Aquarius" at least once. However, most of us have never realized the astronomical significance of this word, and that is particularly true when we read this word in the Bible.

Let's take a look at a few of the times the "month of the great year" comes up. Believe it or not, this is not an exhaustive list. This term gets used quite a bit in the New Testament, mostly by Jesus, Himself:

> *"For inquire, please, of the former age, And consider the things discovered by their fathers;" (Job 8:8)*

> *"Therefore as the tares are gathered and burned in the fire, so it will be at the end of this age." (Matthew 13:40)*

> *"Now as He sat on the Mount of Olives, the disciples came to Him privately, saying, "Tell us, when will these things be? And what will be the sign of Your coming, and of the end of the age?" (Matthew 24:3)*

> *"... teaching them to observe all things that I have commanded you; and lo, I am with you always, even to the end of the age." (Matthew 28:20)*

"... who shall not receive a hundredfold now in this time—houses and brothers and sisters and mothers and children and lands, with persecutions—and in the age to come, eternal life." (Mark 10:30)

"But we speak the wisdom of God in a mystery, the hidden wisdom which God ordained before the ages for our glory." (1 Corinthians 2:7)

"... which He worked in Christ when He raised Him from the dead and seated Him at His right hand in the heavenly places, far above all principality and power and might and dominion, and every name that is named, not only in this age but also in that which is to come." (Ephesians 1: 20 – 22)

"... and have tasted the good word of God and the powers of the age to come... " (Hebrews 6:5)

The passage from Matthew, chapter 24, is a good one to look at to see just how familiar earlier societies were with the ages. The disciples were not scholars or astronomers, yet they had in their everyday vocabulary a word for the 2,100 year progression of time. It shouldn't be lost on us that an "age" was a well known concept to the "man on the street" (if this weren't true, then they could have never asked this question of Jesus... you can't ask questions using terms you don't know). Therefore, asking Jesus about His coming and the end of the age wasn't as vague and mysterious a question as we might imagine. In fact, it was specific and direct. If we can be as familiar with these words as they were, we might start to see a whole drama unfolding in the timely shifts of the ages. We will start to see time again as it was designed.

Let's go back, astronomically speaking, to the time of Adam and Eve. Just going on the Biblical genealogies, it would be about 6,000 years ago. Back then the Spring Equinox was in Taurus. Therefore, the sign of the age that started with the fall of man was the Bull or Ox. So when we look at the earliest cultures and their records, we find religious systems that center around the sacrifice of bulls and oxen. From ancient Greece, to Egypt, to India and beyond, spiritual life was dominated by this sign – and it stayed that way for millennia.

Then, about 2,100 years after the fall of mankind, the age begins to shift again, and Abraham comes on the scene to display the next age. Astronomically speaking, the Spring Equinox was moving into the sign of Aries, which you might recall was a lamb or ram. The first appearance of this sign occurs when Abraham is about to sacrifice his son, Isaac. As the story goes, God intervenes and provides a ram instead. Just a few short centuries after Abraham, Moses institutes an entire sacrificial system that centers on rams and lambs. The sign of Aries was demonstrated in its fullness each Passover when the Israelites sacrificed a pure, spotless lamb. Knowing the sign of the Mazzaroth, and how it changed, even brings a certain rebellion of the Israelites into focus. When Moses was on the mountain receiving the Torah, the people of Israel were worshiping a golden calf (an ox). It wasn't just a return to pagan idolatry, it was a regression in time… a regression in the story.

Nearly 2,100 years later, the age changes again, and this time it's Jesus who displays to the world the sign of the arriving age. For in His day the sign of the age was Pisces – the two fish being bound together and hauled out of the water. Jesus wastes no time proving to the world that He was forwarding the story of time. His first disciples were fishermen, and it doesn't seem long before He is multiplying fish to feed a crowd, or pulling a coin out of a fish's mouth, or meeting the disciples after He rose from the grave – while they were fishing. All of that fishy activity would seem odd for a culture that was traditionally pastoral. Even though Jesus was the "Lamb of God," He made sure to show the world the next chapter of the cosmic story. If we needed more examples, let us look to the first symbol of Christianity – the fish. It would seem the early believers knew very well that the story of Jesus' life, death, and resurrection were the opening acts of their new age. I like to think of them, and the patriarchs like Abraham, as the original (and more accurate) "new agers."

Now, if you're doing the math, you already know that we are nearing the end of this present age. The transition that Jesus marked for us so well was around 2,000 years ago. That means we stand on the verge of moving from the age of Pisces to the age of Aquarius. Turns out, that song from the 70's wasn't wrong. The rest of this book will deal with that very transition and what the age of Aquarius will mean for folks like you and me; but before we end this long introduction, allow me to make just a few more points:

- First, the months of the great year really do act like chapters in a big story. When the cosmic page is turned, it affects the whole earth for the subsequent millennia. So it's not just the stars that are shifting – we are shifting, too. Think of the massive changes felt in the nation of Israel during the last shift. A sect of Judaism, now known as Christianity, was born in the blink of an eye, and then went on to change life on a global scale. On a more somber note, roughly 70 years after the shift, the nation of Israel was besieged by the Romans and the temple, along with its sacrifices, was destroyed. That temple was a prominent feature of the age of Aries, so its destruction says as much about the shift in time as anything. Also, it's always a person (or persons) who is turning the page into the next chapter of the story. It takes an Adam, an Abraham, or a Jesus to close the door on the past and open it to the future. Simply put, it is a human responsibility to tell the time. That makes sense, because the story we are reading is the relational story of God and us. So it is totally appropriate that the celestial drama is reflected in our earthly lives.

- Second, the cosmic clock does more than just mark the transitions and provide a symbol for religious functions; it also explains the *theme* of the age. I think we could make a case that when Abraham started the age of Aries, the story began to focus on the kind of sacrifice that would save us from destruction. The theme of that time was all about a pure offering, culminating in the crucifixion. When Jesus begins to show the signs of the next age, it's all about "catching" people, as you would catch fish. Certainly the last 2,000 years of Christianity have focused on getting people out of the world system and into the boat with God.

- Third, the cosmic clock also shows us a central revelation for each age, and this is found by looking at the sign directly *opposite* the sun. As you know by now, the sign of the age is determined by the position of the sun at the Spring equinox. Well, if you can imagine standing on the sun and looking at the sign the *earth* appeared to be in, you would see the revelatory sign of that age. Later on I'll tell you the origin of these revelatory signs, because that story does a good job of telling us what this fast-approaching next age is all about. For now, take a look at the diagrams to see a thorough view of how the heavenly clock tells the time. Instead of starting with Adam and Eve leaving the garden, let's go back to the age before they fell, when the creation was still perfect.

Figure 4

Prior to the fall, Adam and Eve were in Paradise, the Garden of Eden. The sign for that age was Gemini. The "twins" are Adam and Eve, the first two people in the garden. They shared a perfectly symmetrical relationship. Adam said of Eve, "You are bone of my bone and flesh of my flesh." They were also a perfect reflection (or image) of God, so they looked like a twin in that respect, too. The revelatory sign for this age is none other than Sagittarius. Recall that the archer symbolizes hitting the mark and romantic love. That is what was revealed to them in that age. They were perfect, and they were made to love each other.

Figure 5

When man entered the age of Taurus, the major revelation was death and mortality, represented in the scorpion and serpent. This is, without a doubt, the biggest shift in our collective history. The fall of man was a fall from immortality to mortality. Form eternal life to death. It's hard to believe, but to Adam and Eve the reality (or possibility) of death was the central revelation of the age. The age of Taurus was the age of the fall of mankind.

FIGURE 4

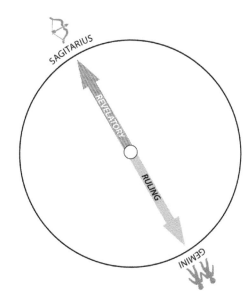

FIGURE 5

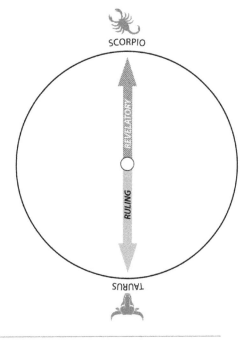

FIGURE 4: The Ruling Sign of Gemini & The Revelatory Sign of Sagitarius
FIGURE 5: The Ruling Sign of Taurus & The Revelatory Sign of Scorpio

FIGURE 6

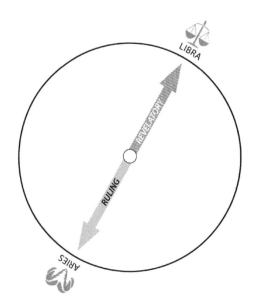

FIGURE 7

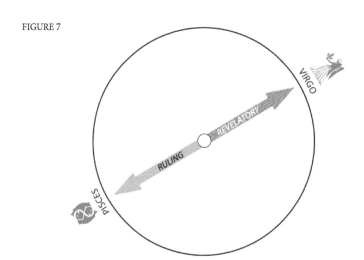

FIGURE 6: The Ruling Sign of Aries & The Revelatory Sign of Libra
FIGURE 7: The Ruling Sign of Pisces & The Revelatory Sign of Virgo

Figure 6

When Abraham transitioned the world into Aries, God reveled to us the Law, shown in the scales of Libra. For about 2,000 years, humanity discovered God's judgments and statutes, primarily through Moses.

Figure 7

Our current age of Pisces is complemented by the sign of Virgo, the virgin woman holding a sheaf of wheat. When Jesus began ordaining "fishers of men," the story shifted to God's desire for a harvest of souls and for the pure, spotless bride. It is no wonder that the church was called the "wife of the Lamb." We could easily say that the Bride of Christ was a central revelation of the last 2 millennia.

Figure 8

In a historically small number of years, we will officially be in the age of Aquarius. The sign of this age is the heavenly, eternal person, pouring out of their vessel rivers of living water. The major revelation of this age will be the return of Jesus, this time as the King – the Lion of the tribe of Judah. In a more general sense, I believe this revelatory sign is for all of us. So, we might say the revelation of this next age will be true human kingship.

FIGURE 8

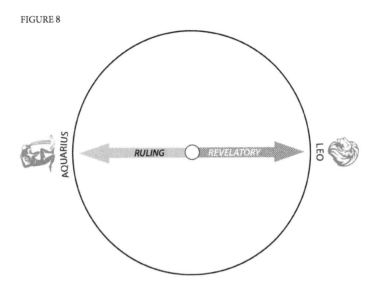

FIGURE 8: The Ruling Sign of Aquarius & The Revelatory Sign of Leo

Part 2:

The Transition

"Life belongs to the living,
and he who lives must be
prepared for changes"

– Johann Wolfgang von Goethe

Therefore, if anyone is in Christ,
he is a new creation; old things
have passed away; behold, all
things have become new.

– 2 Corinthians 5: 17

Chapter 5

Spiritual Revisions

It's important to know that we aren't in the next age yet – but we aren't exactly in the age of Pisces anymore either. This is a time of transition; and just like the ages, themselves, the transitions can take some time. So it's not like a cosmic light switch is flicked on and suddenly we are in the age of Aquarius. Instead, think of it like slowly closing one door while simultaneously opening another. As the door to the age of Pisces is closing, the door to the age of Aquarius is opening, and the time when both doors are open is the transition. This is just my opinion, but I would think a century is a good estimate of the length of a transition on this scale. As you would expect, the transitions are a weird time to be alive, because the flow of the story from both ages is converging on planet earth. Since I believe we are in that moment of flux right now, I also think we should take the time to define a transition. As you would expect after reading the previous chapters, I believe we can look at history to see the future.

> *"Regardless of how all this has changed over the centuries of Christendom, the radical revisions at the turn of the age (and each age) shouldn't be*

overlooked. If we miss this part of the story, we will not be ready when it happens again."

Let's start with the transition from the age of Taurus to the age of Aries. If we were to summarize spiritual life before Abraham, we would have to talk in generalities. Surely there were altars built for worship, and sacrifices have been a part of human/Divine relations since the beginning of human record. As mentioned before, the sacrifice of bulls was common in this period. We could even look to the example of the Tower of Babel, in Genesis 11, to get a sense of religious life in the Age of Taurus. Using that event, we can see that people valued the interaction with Heaven and took interest in interpreting the firmament.

Doubtless there were priests to perform religious duties, but there is a vagueness about religious life in this age when compared to what came after it. As soon as Abraham enters the story and sets apart God's people, the entire direction of spiritual life takes a turn. For it is in this astronomical age that Moses appears and lays out an entire system for temple worship, temple design, religious behavior, and priestly duties. There is no way to overstate the detail of this system.

There are specific details of what kind of sacrifice is used for what. There are instructions on how priests are to serve, right down to the clothes they wear – and that got especially specific. The spiritual responsibilities of the people, best seen in the tithes and offerings made throughout the year, were also specified. And then we have to take into account what constituted worship around the tabernacle and temple. The alter for washing, the alter for burnt offerings, the lighting of the menorah, the care of the Ark, and the function of the feasts and sacrifices were all new things. The presence of the Ark, if nothing else, should give us a sense of how spiritual life changed from the days of Taurus. If you had asked any "Israelite on the street" during the opening centuries of the age of Aries, they would have marveled at how "worship" and "assemblies" had changed since the previous age. While the general concepts of worship and sacrifice were well known since the beginning, the way in which they were done had evolved into something totally different.

If you can imagine taking one of Adam's sons and transporting him across time and space to the time of King Solomon, you might get the sense of what I'm talking about. When Adam's son (let's say Seth just for fun) looked at the temple and the constant activity of priests, not to mention the ornate and purposeful design, he would likely have been quite surprised. Whether he thought the changes were good or bad, he would have to admit that things had indeed changed. Maybe he would say something like, "In my day, we didn't have any of these regulations for worship, and we didn't know about all these feasts! Also, look at how all these priests do a specific job, and who knew that God's presence could be localized in that golden box?!" I'm being a little facetious here, but you get the point – things really changed.

The transition from the age of Aries to the age of Pisces was perhaps even more drastic. Consider Jesus' followers – all Jews – who became the initiators of the new spiritual life of Pisces. All they had known up until their discipleship was the kind of worship I just mentioned, but two things in particular changed the spiritual landscape for generations to come: The first was the advent (and impartation) of the Holy Spirit, which made the assemblies of the early church a far cry from the assemblies around the tabernacle and temple. The presence of the Holy Spirit in the believers made each one capable of interacting with God in worship and service. It's no small leap to call every believer a "royal priesthood"(1 Peter 2:9). The second event was something I mentioned before, the destruction of the temple in 70 AD. To anyone who was following the story, this meant that the sacrifices and priestly service, all fixtures of the previous age, were now impossible to do. To see the center of religious life crumbling to the ground was a severe sign of change. Imagine all the church buildings you are used to seeing suddenly collapse, and you start to get the idea. Spiritual life, as defined in the age of Aries, was no longer even possible in the Age of Pisces.

My favorite way to see this shift is to look at the apostle Paul's letters to the early church. When Paul is teaching them how to conduct their meetings, there are literally no carryovers from the previous age. Sure, the early church met together and worshiped, so the basic function was the same; but how they did it was completely different. Notice that Paul can't quote any passages from the Torah, Psalms, or prophets to tell the first generation of Christians how to have a worship service. He pulls instruction solely from inspiration when he tells them how to let multiple people prophesy and still keep a sense of order. The same is true for instructions on speaking in tongues. Also included are instructions for taking care of the poor and how to conduct oneself at communal meals. You can read most of this in 1 Corinthians 12 if you like.

Before we go on, believe me, I'm not saying the principals of the Torah or the story it told were made obsolete. That cannot be the case not only because it's the sacred scripture but also because that would be the same mistake of disregarding time that we mentioned earlier. What comes before always affects what comes after. It's the practices and the expressions of the story that change so drastically, not the story itself. In other words, the story was still the same, but the characters and their behaviors were wildly different.

To really get this picture, imagine that the next time you showed up for church, the minister said some prayers and then began to sacrifice some doves. Amidst all the shocked faces, I'm sure many would bolt for the doors. But to the people who ushered in this current age of Pisces, it would not have been such a big deal (under the right circumstances, of course). So for them, a New Testament model of worship and assembling was a determined choice. And it was a big one. They made the shift to meet together and do things that were totally unprecedented in the age of Aries. It was their prerogative to practice prophecy, give encouragement, speak in tongues, sing songs, have communal meals, devote themselves to the apostles' teaching, and so on. It was a choice to allow all believers to express the gifts they received from the Holy Spirit. There was room for all of this in a completely new system.

"... animal sacrifices and temple worship would seem totally strange and out of place to a modern churchgoer... and in the same way, modern ("normal") church life will seem totally strange and inappropriate to the believer of the next age."

Let's look at how spiritual organization changed when the age shifted. In Aries, there was a priestly caste of people who performed the duties of the tabernacle and temple. They were the Levites, and the job titles never got more diverse than priest or high priest. Yet again, when Paul is instructing the church on how to administrate in this new sect of Judaism, he doesn't hearken back to any of the former job titles. Instead, he coins terms like apostle, pastor, evangelist, prophet, and teacher. He describes the duties of elders and deacons, which were also new positions. So along with a totally different method of assembly and worship, we get a brand new system of offices and functions. Regardless of how all this has changed over the centuries of Christendom, the radical revisions at the turn of the age (and each age) shouldn't be overlooked. If we miss this part of the story, we will not be ready when it happens again.

Sometimes I marvel at Paul's courage. Even though he stayed connected to the Jewish synagogue and temple, he took an enormous leap when he started revealing spiritual life for the age of Pisces. It must have taken guts to depart from a system in which he was thoroughly trained (remember, at one time Paul persecuted the sect of Christianity on behalf of the Jewish leaders) and embark into totally uncharted waters. In a sense, he had to leave his former practices behind to even call himself an apostle. For, there were no apostles in the age of Aries. What would it take for someone like Paul to let go of his former traditions and formulate totally new ones? What would it take for one of us to let go of the standards we had practiced all our life and take part in a transition of the ages? I think we are about to find out.

In the coming decades, I believe there will be another

revision. Spiritual life in the age of Aquarius will be as different from what is practiced today, as what we do today is different from the age before it. To put it another way, animal sacrifices and temple worship would seem totally strange and out of place to a modern churchgoer (think back to your local minister sacrificing a dove); and in the same way, modern (so called "normal") church life will seem totally strange and inappropriate to the believer of the next age. There is no other way to put it. "Church" (in its now traditional sense) is specific to the age of Pisces. It will not survive (as-is) in the transition any more than the temple and its ordinances survived the last shift.

As an aside, if we find ourselves saying, "That can't be! Church will never pass away! God created it and He wanted it to keep going forever! I refuse to believe that someday there won't be church anymore!" then consider the following: To make those statements is to instantly know how a Jewish person must have felt during the last cosmic transition! Wasn't this the same response many of them had to the suggestion that their practices were limited and needed to be revised? Wasn't this a common response to the entire advent of Christianity?

Chapter 6

Great Commissions

Most church-going folk today are familiar with the commission Jesus gave to His followers. Here it is from the gospel of Matthew:

> *And Jesus came and spoke to them, saying, "All authority has been given to Me in Heaven and on earth. Go therefore and make disciples of all the nations, baptizing them in the name of the Father and of the Son and of the Holy Spirit, teaching them to observe all things that I have commanded you; and lo, I am with you always, even to the end of the age." (Matthew 28: 18, 19)*

This is what many call the "Great Commission", and many Bibles will subtitle this passage with that phrase. Let's remember that the subtitles in your Bible are extremely recent inventions, so it isn't like Jesus started this conversation by saying, "Hey disciples, I'm about to tell you the Great Commission." That term is a bit of a misnomer even though He did, in fact, give them a commission. It's just that this isn't the first time it happened – nor was it the "greatest." If we look back, we can see that this has happened 3 specific times in the story of God and Man. The first commission came with the first transitionary –

Adam. When God established the first man on the earth, He gave him a specific charge:

> *So God created man in His own image; in the image of God He created him; male and female He created them. Then God blessed them, and God said to them, "Be fruitful and multiply; fill the earth and subdue it; have dominion over the fish of the sea, over the birds of the air, and over every living thing that moves on the earth." (Genesis 1: 27, 28)*

The next transitionary we've identified is Abraham, and this is God's commission to him, as found in Genesis, chapter 12, verses 1, 2 and 7:

> *Now the Lord had said to Abram:*
> *"Get out of your country,*
> *From your family*
> *And from your father's house,*
> *To a land that I will show you.*
>
> *I will make you a great nation;*
> *I will bless you*
> *And make your name great;*
> *And you shall be a blessing.*
>
> *Then the Lord appeared to Abram and said, "To your descendants I will give this land."*

Even though God commissions plenty of other people like

David, Moses, and Paul, it is always to do the commission that *started* with a transitionary.

Every time the age changes, we see God giving a new commission for that age, making the one Jesus initiates the 3rd commission. In my opinion, they are actually all "great," and each one vitally important to the progress of humanity – each one carefully chosen, initiated, and charged by God in just the way and time they needed to be presented. They are all *completely necessary* parts of the story. We have a tendency to think the things that are happening in *our* age are the most important things to have ever happened. Therefore, we think the commission that was given for this current age must be *the* "great" one, while the others, if we even believe there are others, must be "lesser" commissions. It's the same belief that would cause an adverse reaction to the statements I made in the last chapter. If you believe the modern "church" as we know it is the evolutionary end of God's plan – the greatest form of assembly and worship that can possibly be attained – then you would be inclined to call it the "greatest" and rail against any suggestion that it was a chapter in the story and nothing more (this is not said to negate its importance, I'm just putting it into context).

It is also interesting how these commissions change the whole direction of the story. Consider that Adam's commission was to fill the whole earth and subdue the whole earth. That meant a lot of expansion. It was a fundamentally outward directive, as there was a lot of earth and living things to subdue. Now think about the charge God gives to Abraham. Instead of attending to the whole earth, Abraham is to gather his people to a very specific plot of land in Canaan. There is a very big difference between filling the earth and congregating a nation on the coast of the Mediterranean. One is outward and expansive, and the other is inward and insular.

Let's think for a moment what would have happened if Abraham tried to do both. What if, instead of heeding the directive to congregate his people, he still tried to fill the earth? It would have been impossible to fulfill the commission of Aries if the Israelites were scattered from the Middle East all the way to British Isles. They needed to be centralized to fulfill their part of the story, which means the commission they received completely trumped the one before it. Or, we could say that the new commission made the old one obsolete.

The same thing is true when Jesus declares the commission for Pisces. Instead of congregating in Israel, the disciples are told to "go into all the world" (the gospel of Mark version). If they were stubborn and held to Abraham's commission, then they would have failed miserably in this new task. There is some evidence they were having that very struggle, because it seems to take some effort for them to actually get out of Jerusalem and take the message to every nation. Further evidence of the confusion could be seen in their fixation on re-establishing the nation of Israel, even though Jesus makes it clear the story is now taking a turn.

Notice, in the first chapter of Acts, the disciples are asking Jesus if He intends to restore the kingdom of Israel. This is actually the last question they ask Him before He ascends to Heaven, which says they still might not have fully grasped the end of the previous commission. Just to reiterate, if the disciples tried to hold onto Abraham's calling – to establish God's nation and government in the land of promise – they would not have been able to fulfill the commission for their own "new" age. The commissions are mutually exclusive.

"As the church grew and included more and more people from the "nations" they were supposed to reach, there is absolutely no effort to conform them to the commission and practices of the previous age."

After 2000 years, it's very easy to take our current commission for granted. It rarely dawns on us how different a direction it must have been for the disciples and early church. Remember, the fathers of Christianity were all Jews. It would have taken a mental and emotional leap to stop thinking something that had been ingrained in their psyche since they were children. The success of the nation of Israel and its restoration was the paramount issue of the day, so to leave that directive behind and focus on getting a message of grace, repentance, and Holy Spirit impartation to the world took some guts. This is a lot like what we said of the apostle Paul in the last chapter. It takes a firm courage to depart from the status quo and do something completely different, but such is the nature of these astronomical transitions.

The early church leaders eventually embraced the change, and we see that in the way they treated the new believing gentiles. As the church grew and included more and more people from the "nations" they were supposed to reach, there is absolutely no effort to conform them to the commission and practices of the previous age. Even though Paul reminds the church of its Hebrew roots, he never returns to Abraham's calling. In fact, he encourages them to look for a "Jerusalem from above" (Galatians 4:26) instead of the Jerusalem in the nation of Israel.

> *"... the age is about to change, and that means we will receive a whole new commission."*

In the same book, Paul denounces anyone who would require converts to fulfill Jewish regulations, like circumcision. Paul isn't the only one to do this sort of thing. The elders in Jerusalem, on hearing of the gentiles' conversion, didn't put any burden on the new believers except some basic guidelines on blood and sexuality. By this point they have moved past the impetus to restore the Jewish nation, and none of their efforts to spread the good news are a veiled effort to reenergize their country. They are spreading the good news without restriction – because they have embraced another commission.

I believe we will face a similar crossroads. The age is about to change, and that means we will receive a whole new commission. In the past, these directives have set the tone for the following 2 millennia. They determined the "why and how" of all our spiritual action. We should take this seriously. We should also consider that what it would require of us is to stop doing something that for 2,000 years has been the standard. We should ponder that even the preaching of the gospel (in the way in which we now know it), which is a wonderful and mighty action, is specific to this quickly closing age. The call to bring that message, and its promises – even the call to estab-lish the church in its wake – only applies to the period of time known as Pisces. Not because we're getting rid of fellowship, gathering together, and communion with God; but because we are able to connect with God in an entirely new way, specific to this new commission!

And, should we miss it, let's not forget that there were no "Hebrews" until Abraham ushered in the age of Aries. There were no "Christians" until Jesus brought us into Pisces. The changes are so drastic that the practitioners of the incoming age don't even identify with the names and titles of the outgoing age. Therefore, it is highly likely, maybe even certain, that the believers of the next age won't even be called Christians. Again, this is not to say that the wealth of restoration, played out in the last 6000 years will be forgotten. May it never be denied! It is simply an indicator that God is not done telling this story, and each chapter is better than the next. Whatever comes after Christianity will be even more glorious than what came before it. Whatever name encapsulates the commission of the next age will be a mark of even more Christlikeness. Given the sign of the next age – the immortal kingship represented in Aquarius and Leo – I'm expecting a wonderful, exciting title for this soon coming commission.

Let's do another personal inventory: If this is frightening or disconcerting to you, then think back to the courage and vision of the church fathers – not to mention their obedience. Aren't we all glad that a small sect of outcast Jews embraced a new commission with a new message? Aren't we glad that they did not force the traditions of the age of Aries on the believing world? I wonder if someone will be grateful for our courage, after this transition has run its course?

Chapter 7

The Transitionaries

"... we should expect groups of people to start living out the next age even before it has properly arrived. Just like John the Baptist and the Essenes, there will be groups and people who practice the next commission and its expressions while this current age has its last hurrah."

So far, we've mentioned the people that officially transitioned the ages – Adam, Abraham, and Jesus – and a few others like Paul who kept the transition going afterwards. As we know, it takes a while for the transition to run its course, maybe even a century or so. Could there be anymore characters playing a part in the transitions, perhaps before the official change begins? For this example, we will look at the shift between Aries and Pisces. We already saw how Jesus officially marked the shift, but look how another important figure takes part in the cosmic changes. We know him as John the Baptist.

... the word of God came to John the son of Zacharias in the wilderness. And he went into all the region around the Jordan, preaching a baptism of repentance for the remission of sins, as it is written in the book of the words of

73

Isaiah the prophet, saying: "The voice of one crying in the wilderness: 'Prepare the way of the Lord; Make His paths straight.

Now as the people were in expectation, and all reasoned in their hearts about John, whether he was the Christ or not, John answered, saying to all, "I indeed baptize you with water; but One mightier than I is coming, whose sandal strap I am not worthy to loose. He will baptize you with the Holy Spirit and fire. (Luke 3: 2 – 16)

Right before Jesus arrives on the scene, John is down by the Jordan River doing some really "next age" things. He baptizes, he preaches repentance, and he acknowledges the Messiah. If you think back, this is the first mention of these kinds of activities in the Bible. That's not bad for someone who isn't even "officially" transitioning the age. Even though he isn't the primary mover and shaker, John still helps to open the next door (the next chapter of the story). It shouldn't be lost on us that he did the "Great Commission" before it had been formally given, and that gives us a historical precedent for people demonstrating the next commission while the sun is setting on the current one. Also, he wasn't the only one to demonstrate this kind of behavior. It is possible we could look to the entire sect of Judaism called the Essenes for more examples. Some scholars have even suggested that John was influenced by this mystical denomination since they also practiced baptism, lived outside of mainstream Judaism, and expected great changes. Additionally, there is some evidence they lived communally, possibly even in remote desert and wilderness areas, which of course is where John the Baptist gets his start.

Whether or not there is a tight connection between the two, the major point is that the change in time was anticipated by more people than just the primary transitionary person. That leads us to the whole point for this chapter. Prior to the shift, we should expect groups of people to start living out the next age even before it has properly arrived. Just like John the Baptist and the Essenes, there will be groups and people who practice the next commission and its expressions while the age of Pisces has its last hurrah. That will make for a pretty interesting sight. On the one hand, we will see devout believers going to church, preaching the words of Jesus, and encouraging baptism. On the other side, there will be an equally devout group of believers that don't do any of these things (or do them sparingly).

Now for the question, "Has this already started to happen?" Yes! It is happening all over the Christianized world. Everywhere I go I meet people who are leaving "church." Yes, sometimes they are disgruntled and frustrated with the systems or traditions of the organized church, but no more than the people who choose to stay. Rather, their disenchantment with Christendom is because of an internal drive towards something brand new. Something unprecedented.

"A radical thought is that one can leave the traditional "church" of this age and not leave the Lord."

It is their unrealized time-sense that pushes many of them into the unknown. Keep in mind that the people who

75

are distancing themselves from the church age of Pisces are no less devout or committed to their heavenly Father! Even if they don't have the words for it, they are moving on *because* of their love for the Creator, for Jesus, and the Holy Spirit not because of a lack of it. A radical thought is that one can leave the traditional "church" of this age and not leave the Lord. But that thought can only survive in a person who senses time as God ordains it. Without a knowledge of the story arc (past and future), someone would think that the church as we now know it is the only thing that ever was or will be. They would believe it to be the sum total of all God *ever* meant to accomplish, and leaving it would be high spiritual treason. But as we've covered in detail by now, the stars – God's appointed time symbols – paint a different picture.

As you've noticed by my use of the word already, I'm choosing to call the people who show their anticipation of the next age by their beliefs and practices "transitionaries." Their job is to be the forerunners of the Aquarius age. They will look ahead to the next commission and start practicing it. They will undoubtably meet together because God's people have always enjoyed assembly; but their meetings will look as different from "church" as the new church looked from the old temple.

This is an important job; but we have to remember that during the transition it's not the only job out there. The commission and practices of Pisces are still valid and prescribed. Even more, they are dear to the heart of God. It would be profoundly foolish for forerunners to think their job is more important or that they are of some kind of "elite" – or to judge those who are fulfilling their mission for this current age in its usual, prescribed practices as not being forward thinking. On the other hand, it would be equally foolish for the believers focused on the practices of Pisces to impede those reaching forward into the next age.

"Remember that the apostle Paul and the early church leaders didn't expect the blossoming gentile congregations to worship in the temple or synagogue. Quite to the contrary, they did the opposite. They gave them the room to do something completely different – something far removed from the practices of their previous age."

In an effort to smooth over some of these "new waters" let me give a word of advice to the church: Please don't require the transitionaries of the next age to assimilate into the "church" life of the age of Pisces. Remember that the apostle Paul and the early church leaders didn't expect the blossoming gentile congregations to worship in the temple or synagogue. Quite to the contrary, they did the opposite. They gave them the room to do something completely different – something far removed from the practices of their previous age. So let's expect the transitionaries of the coming age to do some different things. Let's expect them to focus less on preaching the gospel (as we now know it) and planting churches, even though those issues are foundational and beloved. Let's expect them to herald a message that's completely grounded in the story of God and Man as we've read in the Bible, but one that also introduces new subject matter.

It is entirely possible that the transitionaries will be considered strange and outcast because of these new things, and once again history can give us many examples of that. In the last transition the outcast Jews were hated and persecuted even to death. It's too early to tell if this transition will be embraced or feared, so I'm not going to get gloomy just yet. For now, I think it would suffice if we were at least open minded to these ideas. Just to recap, the ideas I've presented so far go something like this:

- While we go around believing time to be very important and central to our lives, the essence and meaning is missing. Consequently, we might be blind to the context of the story of God and Man. Without this story arc, we wouldn't know that our current chapter is nearing its end and there is still more story to tell!

- The firmament was created to tell the story and mark our place in it. The Mazzaroth gives us the building blocks for understanding time and the ages.

- The ages change; and with those changes come new commissions and new spiritual practices. Often these changes in spiritual direction are quite drastic. *I believe we are in the transition period between ages right now.*

- During the transition between ages, it is possible to see both the old and new commissions demonstrated. The people who anticipate the next age (like John the Baptist or the Essenes) will begin exploring the next chapter of the story, and might even gracefully bow out of the previous age and its practices. These people could be called "transitionaries."

Part 3:

Finding Immortal Life

"I have come home at last! This is my real country! I belong here. This is the land I have been looking for all my life, though I never knew it till now... Come further up, come further in!"

– C.S. Lewis, *The Last Battle*

For this perishable body must put on the imperishable, and this mortal body must put on immortality.

– 1 Corinthians 15:53

Chapter 8

Eternal Dimensions

From an early age I was fascinated with astronomy – I even went on to study it in college. However, nothing I read in a textbook or saw through a telescope could have given me the picture of time and the firmament that we've been talking about. I learned all of that from an entirely different source, and now's the time for me to tell you how that happened. Just so you have a little background, I was raised in a Christian home and knew what it meant to pray. In fact, I prayed a lot throughout my life. After some experiences during my college years I was familiar with the idea of God showing me something during prayer. It might have been a flash of a picture in my mind, a dream, or even a prolonged vision.

All that is to say I did have a framework for seeing things that weren't necessarily in my so-called earthly reality. But whatever I thought I knew about God's desire to communicate and His methods for doing it changed some years ago when my spiritual eyes were opened even further. I began seeing in a way I never expected, and instead of a flash of a picture or a vision of something, I started to perceive Heaven as if I was actually there. Turns out I was actually there, or at least my spirit was! There is no way I can cover in this book all the details of my journey of discovering how to literally walk in the heavenly realm with Jesus, or tell you how to start experiencing Heaven in the Spirit for yourself. Nor can I go into all the proofs for why this phenomenon is Biblically prescribed and encouraged in this book. I can only encourage you to look into two other books I've written on the subject: *Caught Up in the Spirit* and *In the Palaces of Heaven*.

Dear Reader, I promise this is no cheap attempt at product placement. It is my genuine desire that you learn to interact with the Lord and His Heavens in the Spirit, and this is the best way I know to get you started. So if you're unfamiliar with the concept of being "in the Spirit" like the Apostle John in the book of Revelation, or if you'd like to know what Paul was talking about when he was "caught up to Heaven," then please read those two volumes. The phenomenon of being in the heavenly dimensions in the Spirit is a crucial component of this book, and I don't want it to be a mystery for you. It is the sole reason any of this information is being propagated. If you don't have access to the aforementioned works, then just keep reading with discernment and faith. Since the information in this book is revelatory and sometimes theoretical, reading with discernment is a necessity in any case. And, if it all seems a little "out of this world," then just know that it felt the exact same way to me when it happened. Overall, I think it's important that you know how I received this. Everything in this book, from the cosmic ages to the theories I will present later, all came from participating in the heavenly dimension. Here's the rest of the story of how it started...

It began with long encounters with Jesus and my heavenly Father, and it was very common in those early days for the Lord to actually take me to the Garden of Eden, one of His many courtrooms, or the heavenly city – the New Jerusalem. We went to libraries, and even to a school where I spent some quality time getting used to seeing the heavenly realm. I had always had an expectation of Heaven. I think every believer does. Jesus' promise to the thief on the cross that "today you will be with me in Paradise," is something that we all take kind of seriously.

Like most everyone else, I held those future realities dear and thought of them as something to look forward to. You can imagine my surprise when I started seeing and walking in those places before I was dead and in the ground! But the ability to see the eternal, glorious environs of Heaven, and from that place enjoy a two-way, unhindered conversation with my heavenly Dad was an ultimate blessing. I was hooked from the start. This was, without a doubt, the single greatest revolution of my life – and continues to be to this day.

For the first two years I observed the heavenly dimension, I was continually struck by a disconcerting truth – what I was seeing in the Spirit was real. It wasn't just a figment of my imagination. Often, the actions of my "spirit man" in the heavenly dimension directly affected my environs in the earthly dimension! With every miraculous encounter, I became more and more convinced that my prayer times "in the Spirit" were introducing me to a world just as substantial and solid – in fact, more so – than my earthly home. This mortal world is decaying away, after all, and the things I was observing in Heaven were everlasting. They had to be more substantial by default! See the verse below for a good affirmation of this:

"Do not lay up for yourselves treasures on earth, where moth and rust destroy and where thieves break in and steal; but lay up for yourselves treasures in Heaven, where neither moth nor rust destroys and where thieves do not break in and steal. For where your treasure is, there your heart will be also. (Matthew 6: 19 - 21)

Also, in the beginning I was doing good to just see or hear in the heavenly realm, and I could only maintain my spiritual concentration for short periods.

As the months passed however, I could not only see and hear, but smell and feel. All my senses started firing as my spirit explored another dimension. It was always clear that it was my spirit – and not my mortal body – doing the traveling. But over time what was happening in my Spirit was starting to feel real and tangible – as if my actual biological cells were somehow taking part. To give you some examples, there were times when Jesus and I would share a meal, and I could actually taste the food and feel its textures in my mouth. Or there were times when He would grab my hand and I would feel an electric jolt pass through my body.

The problem with all the development was a dumbstruck confusion when I would come out of my prayer time and go back to living in my mortal body. A good summary of the confusion goes like this: There is clearly a heavenly dimension (again, this is a Biblical no-brainer. Of course there is a Heaven. I just never expected to experience it before I die). That dimension is glorious and eternal. Nothing is dying there, and when I'm there, I also feel glorious and eternal. It felt like every time I went in the Spirit, I shed my mortal life with its corruptions and weaknesses and experienced a wholly restored existence.

Then, of course, there was my life in my mortal, failing body. That life is lived on a fallen earth, where everything slowly marches towards death and disintegration. A fundamental law of Physics is that everything moves towards disorder and chaos. Everything degenerates (check out thermodynamics if you're interested in this sort of thing). So on the one hand I had a heavenly experience that I much preferred, and on the other hand I had an earthly existence that was clearly fallen. Both were real, but the things I discovered in Heaven were clearly more real, since they are more substantial and everlasting. To make matters more troubling, simply admitting that I was sensing two very different dimensions (and that I wanted to live in the one that you can't see with your biological eyes) was like admitting lunacy. What was I to do?

My fearful response was to bow out for a short season to take a short break from going to Heaven. Yet after a few months the tension was still there. Even though I was pretending I didn't know it was possible to access a dimension that was much more favorable than fallen earth, I still was very aware that it existed. I weighed it out over and over again, trying to get over fears of what people might say or perhaps losing touch with an earthly reality (for what it's worth, that might actually be a good thing). The final analysis was that there was no going back, and pretending to forget this discovery was not going to work. So one evening I sat down with the intent to visit Heaven in the Spirit and let my heavenly Father know that I had thought it through and I wanted to keep going. Not surprisingly, He had anticipated my decision that night.

Once I started looking with my spiritual eyes, Jesus took me to the heavenly dimension where I saw a small table for two, with a white tablecloth draped over it. On the table were two settings of fine, white china and a slender vase filled with blue flowers. I could see Jesus standing next to the table, and my immediate impression was that we were going to sit down and have a chat, probably in response to me getting over my fears of being in Heaven.

When I sat down He remained standing. Then I saw a woman sit down across from me in the other chair. From what I could see around the flowers, I made out a woman dressed in white and blue, and with long dark hair. Out of curiosity I moved the vase to the side to see her better. What I saw then took my breath away. The woman was so beautiful and regal. She even seemed to radiate white and blue light. Her features were all highlighted, from her warm smile to her dark hair. And on top of her head was a bright crown lined with diamonds and sapphires. I knew who she was even without asking. It was as if her name radiated out from her with the light. It was Mary, the mother of Jesus, and I could see why she said of herself that "all generations will call me blessed"(Luke 1:48). Before anything else happened, I remember thinking, "If Mary is an example of what will happen to us when we are totally restored, then we are going to be really blessed!"

At that moment, Jesus looked at us and said, "I'll give you two a few minutes to talk," and then He walked away. I was in a stunned silence because I was used to Jesus taking me by the hand and guiding me around in the Spirit. It was very unusual for Him to leave me, even for a second. Yet here I was sitting with Jesus' mother while He took a stroll. I had no idea what to say. What, after all, do you say to the mother of Jesus? I often look back on this moment and laugh at myself, but given the decision I had just made concerning my life in the heavenly dimension, all I could think to say was, "Why me?" In truth, I was really wondering why all of this was happening to me, and she seemed so maternal and safe that it just felt like the right thing to ask. With her warm smile she simply answered, "You know, I asked Him the same thing about myself."

At this point I might have done a face-palm slap and marveled at my own lack of perception – of course she asked that. This is the woman who was told she would bear a child, even though she was a virgin, and that child would be God in the flesh. If ever a person in the history of the world had the right to ask, "Why me?" it was her. My small internal tension hardly seemed important anymore. However, Mary didn't use this moment to say, "Buck up, pal. I had it worse than you." Rather, she encouraged me and even told me the Lord's response to her when she asked that common question. She said the only answer she ever got out of Him was, "Because I chose you." We talked for a few minutes more while she offered her gentle affirmations that made a world of difference to me. And then, as promised, Jesus came back to the table.

After I parted company with Mary, Jesus took me to another place in Heaven where I met a special angel. Again, I have to point you to the aforementioned books to get the whole story, but the quick version is that this angel came to be a close friend. The angel's name was Breanadan. As it turned out, he was a wonderful heavenly navigator, and he taught me how to get around the Heavens on my own. In other words, I didn't need someone holding my hand the whole time. Also, he introduced me to a whole family of angels that quickly became regular company on my heavenly visits. With the increase of freedom in the heavenly dimension also came an increased sense of belonging. I was getting to know the angels, I was seeing and sensing more clearly than ever, and it all felt so right. Then, as if to punctuate these months of progress after I met Mary, the Lord brought me to my eternal inheritance.

I was brought to a glorious palace perched on a cliff side and overlooking the ocean. I couldn't have imagined a more idyllic setting. At first I didn't even know it was my home. I thought I was just visiting another heavenly place, or perhaps the home of an angel. But with great pride, the Lord, and the angels I had come to call friends, showed me around this house and pointed out all the things that were made just for me. To put this in context, I had been wandering around Heaven with the Lord and the angels for years by this time. Having a home that was just for me, and that I could return to effortlessly, was one of the greatest developments of my heavenly journey. It grounded me and gave me a true sense of belonging. It made it far easier to call that dimension my true, eternal home.

It was in this home, in my library overlooking a cliff and an ocean, that I began to learn about the stars. My angelic friends were there, along with the Apostle John and an ever-present Jesus. One of the angels took a book off the shelf called *Stars for All Seasons*. For weeks we looked through that book while the angels taught me about the firmament. Everything I have learned about time – the Cosmic Clock, the revelatory signs, the ages, and the transitions – I learned in Heaven. It all came from time spent in my heavenly home, letting the Lord and His angels teach me while reading incorruptible books that are incapable of collecting dust and fading.

Chapter 9

Forerunners

It's a strange and radical proposition – the idea of living in two dimensions that couldn't be more dissimilar. But this may be the very first step of any transitionary towards the next age. Let me give a brief explanation why. Anyone who is reaching towards the next age will be reaching to a time when immortal people will be living their fully restored and glorified life. Remember that this next transition will be preceded by a return of Jesus, and that in the words of the Apostle Paul, Jesus will resurrect "those who are Christ's at His coming" (1 Corinthians 15: 23). Therefore, no matter what comes in the next age, it must include people who have completed the story of the redemption of man and have moved on to the next chapter of human and divine development.

If we think back to the sign of the next age, we can see this development painted in the stars. The Aquarius is, after all, a heavenly person, often depicted with wings like an angel. It is a sign of a completed man, one who has finished living out the story of human restoration. The transitionaries will take the first steps into that life and its commission, which means they must take steps into the eternal realms of Heaven. My journey that I recounted to you in the last chapter is just one example of a transitionary beginning the journey to a heavenly, immortal life. There are many, many others.

"Interestingly, this has not been the primary focus of our current age, even though it was a hallmark of the first Christians. Why or how we stopped talking about our access to Heaven is buried in the history somewhere."

As exciting as this first step may seem, it is also the source of some tension. We have with us right now the ability to perceive and be conscious in the eternal dimensions of Heaven, but we also live in a body that seems a long way off from inheriting that glory. It leaves us with only one choice, and that is to experience the heavenly realms now in the Spirit, and wait for our bodies to catch up. Who knows how long that might take, but I will make a few comments on this before we finish this section. For now, I'd like to look at those who foresaw this happening. I think it will encourage the transitionaries that the upward call they feel was predicted, and in the first case – experienced.

To begin, let's look back to Jesus. Tucked away in a passage that most of us know for it's often repeated statement of "for God so loved the world," is a sentence or two about dimensional matters.

If I have told you earthly things and you do not believe, how will you believe if I tell you heavenly things? No one has ascended to Heaven but He who came down from Heaven, that is, the Son of Man who is in Heaven. (John 3: 12 – 13)

We might have just caught Jesus giving away something very important. The last line of this passage is an admittance that while His body is on the earth, His persona is also in Heaven. In my previous books I wrote about this phenomenon, and how the early church leaders like Paul and John also experienced living in two dimensions. But I find it fitting that the process of becoming transdimensional was first put forth by the great transitionary, Himself. He was the first to put into words that a person could be in two dimensions at the same time. So from the very beginning of the age of Pisces, the end was already in sight.

Interestingly, this has not been the primary focus of our current age, even though it was a hallmark of the first Christians. Why or how we stopped talking about our access to Heaven is buried in history somewhere. But like all the parts of the story, they have their appointed time. Currently, there is a resurgence in talk about Heaven and people telling their true stories about going there. More and more people are realizing their access to the "heavenly places," and I think that's leading somewhere. What if the beginnings of experiencing Heaven in the Spirit were just that – the beginnings? In other words, the seeds were planted at the beginning of Pisces, but they will produce their greatest fruit at the end of this age and in the age to come.

There are two (now somewhat obscure) voices in the last century I'd like to draw your attention to who foresaw this resurgence of perceiving Heaven in the Spirit. The first is the British philosopher, author, and poet, Owen Barfield. I would encourage reading his book, *Saving the Appearances*, to get to know his line of thinking better. Also, it would be helpful to know of his associations with C.S. Lewis, a celebrated Christian author. Lewis called Barfield, the "wisest and best of my unofficial teachers," so there is likely something to be gleaned from his contributions. For myself, I discovered Barfield's work after years of exploring the Heavens, and I found his thoughts on imagination very refreshing. Barfield knew that there was more to life than just what we could see with our biological eyes. Also (I'm really simplifying his words here), he understood that we would have to use our imagination to see those other things.

In our present day the word "imagination" has come to mean something more like "fantasy." In other words, it refers to something that isn't real. Barfield, on the contrary, goes to great lengths to affirm the imagination as something God given and necessary for perceiving a true reality, which includes everything in the heavenly dimension. In my own life, I have found this to be true. While I maintain that the gift of the Holy Spirit was responsible for opening my eyes to the heavenly realms, the eyes that were opened were none other than the eyes of my imagination. It is a terrible shame how this word has lost its potency and has become almost laughable. I'll say more on this later, but for now just consider how much of our sacred art, literature, or music comes from the imagination within. How is it that we have figured the eternal, unseen things at all, throughout history, if not for our inspired imaginations?

Before we move on to another prophetic voice, just consider that Barfield thought that any step forward must include (in his words) "an attempt to use imagination systematically." And later on in his book *Saving the Appearances,* Barfield states that "Iconoclasm is made possible by the seed of the Word stirring within us, as imagination." If we think of Iconoclasm as the drastic reordering and restructuring that accompanies a transition of ages, then we can see why Barfield's voice is prophetically accurate.

For the transitionaries, the unavoidable pull towards the heavenly dimension must first be experienced in the internal eyes of our imagination. This is as good a definition as any of what it means to be "in the Spirit." Or maybe we could say it this way – that being in the Spirit is using our imagination in a way that has been sanctioned and sanctified by the Holy Spirit. It is also safe to say that we must practice being in the Spirit, and this is where the "systematic" approach comes in. Anyone who tries to connect with their eternal home finds out very quickly that it takes a disciplined practice to get comfortable with it – myself included. It is not immediately easy to allow your consciousness to flow with the Holy Spirit in the heavenly dimension (that might be a huge understatement). The encouragement here is that Barfield foresaw all of that and also predicted the use of our internal, Holy Spirit empowered eyes as the first step to be taken towards the next commission. In his words, the next drastic restructuring (Iconoclasm) would be "made possible" by an inspired imagination.

Owen Barfield left this earth in 1997, and ten years later Heaven gained another prophetic voice worth mentioning – Arthur Katz. Art was an American Jewish Christian who preached and authored books right up until he died in 2007. Just as with Barfield, I think everyone would be enriched by reading his books. And also like Barfield, Art Katz was never quite mainstream. These two voices stayed on the fringe of Christianity, and that may be the very reason why they were able to peer around its middle to see what was coming after the age of Pisces had run its course. Just to reiterate; seeing past the age of Pisces is akin to seeing past the time of the "church" as we now know it. Fringe worthy material, indeed.

To get a sense of how important all this was to Art, I'll include a few of his statements from his book *Apostolic Foundations*. I confess that I had read this book almost 10 years before I started visiting Heaven in the Spirit myself. It never dawned on me that what Art was saying could become an actual experience. I think that most of us, and maybe even Art Katz, himself, didn't quite know what we were getting ourselves into. As we've already discussed, time has its way with things, and the phenomenon of "transdimensionalism" awaited an appointed time at the end of this age to come into its own. In my opinion, that makes Art's words all the more prophetic, since he likely never had a full understanding of what he wrote. Here are some pertinent excerpts:

The foundation of the apostolic mind-set is a true apprehension of the things that are eternal, not in anticipation of a future enjoyment, but of a present appropriation.

Here, Art is speaking about Eternity...

We are going to have to contend for this word because the world is not hospitable to it. Paul not only found this eternal dimension, he also dwelt in it, and yet that did not condemn him to irrelevancy. On the contrary, it made him all the more relevant, and so will it make us also.

On the difficulty of seeing the eternal dimension...

The issue of seeing is crucial, and I know it is going to take a conscious and concerted effort to bring us to this kind of seeing. Everything presently conspires against it. The world wants to fill our eyes... Everything is clamoring for the attention of our senses. We are continually bidden to look down upon things.

About living in the heavenly dimension...

We need to come to the world as people who are presently in that dimension, where the things that are eternal are brought into our daily, mundane and ordinary considerations.

So if I summarize Jesus' words along with these two (in my opinion) under-appreciated prophets, I might say they paved the way for the transitionaries like this: They showed us that what the world thinks about the imagination is a far cry from what it really is. They showed us that from the very onset of the age of Pisces, there has been a push towards transdimensionalism. They showed us the importance of a heavenly consciousness as a precursor of any next age activity. And finally, they both agree that it will take some determined practice.

To put it another way, this is their message to the Aquarius transitionaries:

- In order to demonstrate the life of a heavenly, immortal, and glorified person, we must first learn to live in that glorious, eternal dimension from right where we are – right now. Secondly, we will need to devote a great deal of time and effort to this pursuit.

Chapter 10

Letting Go

Have you ever had a "point of no return?" I think most people have had at least one moment in life when a decision carried this kind of weight. It is normally accompanied by some fear and uncertainty, but also excitement and anticipation. That is exactly the way I felt when I made the decision to pursue the heavenly dimension and never look back. I described that moment to you a few chapters ago, and how the Lord and His mother waited for me to make that decision. I also spoke to you briefly about what happened afterwards, for as soon as I made that leap, I began relating to angels and discovered my own heavenly dwelling place.

Sometimes I think of the years of wandering around Heaven in the Spirit as just the preparation for that moment. Truly, something amazing happens when a person decides to leave their mortal life behind and press on to eternal realms. I'm reminded of the verse of an old hymn, "and the things of the earth will grow strangely dim... "

"... immortality and glory were the original state
of man – and rediscovering it feels like finally
coming home."

99

This is what awaits any transitionary who begins to live in the heavenly dimension. In that glorious realm, there is access to all the angelic orders, along with the entire family of God who are present with Him in His paradise. There are books to read and classes to attend. Don't worry, I can promise that any education in Heaven would never be described as boring. To me, it feels more like a roller-coaster ride because the information stretches my brain to the limits. I'd also like to point out that the treasures of wisdom up there are very personalized. I learned about time and the firmament because those are things that I was created to love. Others will discover the nature and purpose of creation in ways that reflect who they are.

Then there are the times of fellowship. What a wonderful treasure to simply walk around the Garden with my heavenly Father! If this were the only experience to be had in the Spirit, it would still be more than enough! However, since our Father celebrates abundance, it never stops there. Just when you think you're completely peaceful and satisfied beyond measure, He takes you to a heavenly feast where you meet a saint you've read about in the Bible. Or perhaps He shows you another aspect of the home He has created for you, and that in turn leaves you feeling like the most favored person ever created. I could go on, but suffice it to say that immortality and glory were the original state of man – and rediscovering it feels like finally coming home.

Realistically speaking, this takes some "letting go." It takes some determination to drop the anchors connecting us to a fallen earth and find a more substantial reality. But, no matter the challenges, it is readily available; and I'm speaking from personal experience here. No matter what the person's background, spiritual history, or culture, I've never encountered someone who just couldn't do this. Sure, it can be hard getting started for some folks, but God isn't offering this to an elite. It is available to everyone.

This isn't surprising. It is clear both Biblically and in practice that the Lord wants a real and tangible relationship with His children. An offer to join Him in Heaven is exactly the kind of thing He would do – just read John 14:3. And when someone takes that offer and has the courage to begin living in the eternal dimension, a whole other world opens up to them. Again, speaking from personal experience, I have watched many people befriend angels, find their eternal inheritance, learn things both cosmic and archaic, and ultimately – be transformed.

Now, about the "letting go" part; it might help us to see what we're up against. If we were to take in the tenor of the present time, circa 2014, we will see some alarming trends. Just go to any shopping mall in America and do a little people watching to get a glimpse of what's happening. Everywhere you look there are people looking at screens. Smartphones and iPads top the list. I'm amazed that more people don't run into each other, because it's just as common a practice while walking (or driving for that matter) as when sitting down! The Facebook updates, the Instagram posts, and the texts are as ubiquitous as air.

"So if this sort of thing continues, the western world (certainly America) will be full of people who are increasingly aware of technology and desperately out of touch with the creation. This is dangerous ground."

So what's the problem with all that you might ask? Well, it's causing everyone to keep looking down. Look at someone glued to their smartphone and you will see someone looking down at a screen. Watch a habitual texter and you'll see a detachment from the natural surroundings – like the sky – which we've already pointed out is being taken for granted.

On one occasion while hosting some friends at our house, my wife and I marveled that of the 6 people in the room, we were the only two not looking at some kind of device. As a sort of experiment we waited to see how long it would take before people put down the screens and talked to each other. In short, the screens won, and we had to intervene to bring back some non-electronic communication. So if this sort of thing continues, the western world (certainly America) will be full of people who are increasingly aware of technology and desperately out of touch with the creation. This is dangerous ground.

Conversely, when a person begins to peer into the eternal realm in the Spirit, they are looking up into more dimensions than the 4 we are familiar with on this fallen earth (3 spatial dimensions and 1 time dimension). Seeing into Heaven requires seeing beyond the limits of those dimensions that define earthly space. You could say that when you are looking at Heaven you are looking at higher dimensions.

Now compare that to what we've just been talking about. When you are looking at a screen, you are looking at something in 2 dimensions. No matter how much depth appears in the graphics, a screen only has a length and width, so you have to look down, dimensionally speaking. Who knows what effect "looking down" will have over time, but it's disconcerting to say the least. At a time when the firmament is telling us to learn to look up into Heaven, the world is being trained to constantly look down. Does that sound like a dastardly, evil plan or what?

Unfortunately, the picture gets even bleaker when we factor in television. One recent statistic states that the average American watches over 5 hours of TV per day. Over the course of a lifetime, that adds up to almost 10 years. 10 years! That's 10 years that someone could have been perceiving – even living in – Heaven! If I offered anyone a chance to spend 5 hours each day in Heaven (which they were obviously not using for work or social interaction), don't you think they would jump at the chance?

The obvious difference in these two experiences is that it takes some practice and commitment to observe Heaven, and it takes no work at all to watch television. That brings us to an interesting point: It will always seem easier to look down into less – or lower – dimensions than it is to look up into eternity. I liken it to walking up and down stairs. It's definitely easier going down. We will have to fight this trend if we hope to make progress towards the next age and its commission.

Sometimes I think of these screens, whether it's a smartphone, TV, or a computer, as a window into another world – a less substantial world. And there's one more example of this worth mentioning. Keeping up with the digital trend is the popularity of "ebook readers." As you know, these devices replace an actual, physical book. Don't get me wrong. Ebooks can be a huge blessing to people in certain situations. Vision challenges, being unable to read during daylight hours or in proper light, having a minuscule book budget... there are many circumstances when the creation of ebooks can mean the difference between someone reading or not reading some valuable texts. The plethora of free and exceedingly cheap collections of classic literature, hard to find works, independent writers, and the valuable, rare (and often scholarly) works that are now out of print but are suddenly accessible to us through the creation of ebooks is a gift, indeed.

But for the sake of continuing the argument of the current age being more engaged on a digital level than a "real" level, I came across an article in "Scientific American" magazine that took a look at reading in this new, digital age. Not surprisingly, most studies suggest we don't read as well, or retain as much information, when reading off a screen. Think about the experience of holding a book, turning the pages, and processing the information in multiple dimensions and with multiple senses. Now, consider an ebook. No smell of paper. No texture on the binding. No depth. It still qualifies as reading, but it is reading in less dimensions.

Isn't everything richer the higher up you go? Aren't 3-D images more life-like than 2-D? Isn't everyday life, experienced in 4 dimensions, fuller and richer than anything you have ever seen on a screen? I think we would all answer "yes" to those questions, but it would seem the whole world is on a path to life in less dimensions, even though we know better. Just to put things in perspective, consider again the difference in reading a 2-D ebook vs. a 3-D physical book. Now, imagine reading a book in Heaven, where you would be reading in more (or higher) dimensions. I would expect that kind of reading to be even richer than anything experienced on this earth, and that was exactly how I felt when reading books about the firmament in my heavenly library.

"It's as if our understanding of the lower 4 dimensions trumps any understanding of things in higher dimensions. Shouldn't it be the other way around?"

As we discussed earlier, the idea of using one's imagination to do anything in a higher dimension is almost laughable these days. So transitionaries should expect some backlash from a society and a church body that has bought into the current thinking. In this way, it's not unlike the degradation of time we talked about in the first chapters. We saw how God, Himself, acknowledges that the constellations have an influence on the earth, but modern thinking would scoff at the notion. "How can the stars, which are nothing more than flaming balls of gas separated by thousands of light years, have any effect on us?" It's as if our understanding of the lower 4 dimensions trumps any understanding of things in higher dimensions. Shouldn't it be the other way around?

The world assumes that the imagination can't be real because it doesn't perceive things in the 4 dimensions we know. People might say, "It's all in your head." Or possibly, "You're just making it up." I offered in the first chapters that our modern, mathematical, and objective view of time lacks meaning and substance, and that it has dire consequences. I would offer that the same thing has happened to our view of imagination. It has become meaningless. Shear fantasy and daydreaming. Not anything like the "eyes of the heart" for which the apostle Paul prays. It's a strange sort of arrogance to assume that the last 200 years or so of development and knowledge should trump the holistic wisdom of the previous 6,000 years. Yet at this moment the world is trading in its imagination – the ability to see into higher dimensions – for a mere television screen.

> *"All of the devotion to television and internet activity could be a massive cry for help. It seems as if the population is looking for another world, and they are frantically seeking it in the lower dimensions."*

None of these things are unbeatable, but they will require a "letting go." I'm not saying that there isn't a place for movies and texting. In fact, I quite enjoy watching certain things on TV. It's the overall trend that is problematic. If the world is racing towards life in less dimensions, then any transitionary reaching up into more will be going against the flow. The pressure is always there to conform or compromise. So the pressure will come on two fronts: The first is internal. There will be a moment (if not many) when a transitionary will have to decide if looking up to Heaven is even a sane proposition. The second source will come from the trends of society. Both are a mighty struggle.

As a final note of encouragement, let's look at those trends from a different perspective. All of the devotion to television and internet activity could be a massive cry for help. It seems as if the population is looking for another world, and they are frantically seeking it in the lower dimensions. My guess is that they aren't satisfied. Also, take into account the increase in online gaming over the years. Millions of people create a life for themselves inside these games, and for some it is all consuming. Taken as a whole, I'd say people are looking for a different reality. Might they be sensing the time? Might they be feeling the pull to a higher dimensional presence? Is it possible they are transitionaries just waiting to get out, but no one has told them to look dimensionally *up*, instead of down?

Chapter 11

The Enoch Generation

Do you wonder what would happen to a person if they continued to pursue the heavenly dimension? What if someone practiced seeing and living in the heavenly dimension for decades? Where would that lead? There are a few examples from the Bible we should consider, because I think the question of "How does all this heavenly interaction change us?" is a good one. First, I always like looking back to Enoch. You can read about him in Genesis, chapter 5; and in the New Testament in Hebrews, chapter 11. Enoch is famous because he ascended to Heaven without dying, making him just one of a few people in history to pull that off. As the story goes, Enoch was just 7 generations from Adam and probably still had a very keen sense of what life could be like on the other side of the gate to the Garden of Eden. So he dedicates 300 years to walking with God before he is able to ascend to the eternal realm – and the eternal garden – for good.

> *"What's pertinent here is that his 300 years of walking with God had a profound effect on his ability to go to the immortal dimension, body and all. So maybe there are more far reaching effects of spending time in Heaven other than the already awesome increases in relationship with God, His angels, and the mysteries of the cosmos."*

I imagine over the course of 300 years he developed quite the familiarity with the heavenly dimension while he walked with the Creator, which explains why he was able to make such a smooth leap to the other realm. Since he wasn't that far removed from the gate to the Garden, chronologically speaking, maybe he was not that far away from it spatially. This is just my own pondering, but what if Enoch knew where that gate was and hung around it long enough to soak up some of the heavenly glory on the other side? It's possible he even went back in, and that's where he was walking and talking with the Father for those 3 centuries. Either way, he was reaching for the other dimension (the book of Hebrews says he did this by his faith) and that had some interesting effects on his life and death (or lack thereof).

What's pertinent here is that his 300 years of walking with God had a profound effect on his ability to go to the immortal dimension, body and all. So maybe there are more far reaching effects of spending time in Heaven other than the already awesome increases in relationship with God, His angels, and the mysteries of the cosmos. But before we go there, let's look at a few other examples. We see another Enoch like journey to Heaven with the prophet Elijah. Arguably, his dimensional journey was more dramatic, because the book 1 Kings tells us that a chariot of fire came to pick him up when it was time to go to the eternal realm. Just like Enoch, there was no actual death. Something about Elijah had already prepared him for the glory and energy of Heaven; so when he left, he could do so in his body. Like Enoch, could he have been reaching up to Heaven while walking around this fallen earth?

It's hard to exclude Jesus from a list of supremely transdimensional people, but for the moment we have to. Even though Jesus ascended to Heaven in His body, He did so after dying an actual death. Beating death (because of a heavenly life) is even cooler than skipping death in my book! For now, let's focus on people who go bodily into Heaven without dying. Biblically speaking, there are only two historical examples, Enoch and Elijah, but take a look at this statement from the apostle Paul about what's coming.

For this we say to you by the word of the Lord, that we who are alive and remain until the coming of the Lord will by no means precede those who are asleep. For the Lord Himself will descend from Heaven with a shout, with the voice of an archangel, and with the trumpet of God. And the dead in Christ will rise first. Then we who are alive and remain shall be caught up together with them in the clouds to meet the Lord in the air. (1 Thessalonians 4: 15 – 17)

What we have here is a future moment when everyone who is "in Christ" is suddenly glorified and joined with Jesus. Note that the dead are raised and then everyone still living is "caught up" also. That means that anyone still living when Jesus returns will not experience death – ever. They will go from a mortal existence to an eternal, glorified one in a moment, not unlike Enoch and Elijah.

Some time ago, the Lord proposed a question to me. He asked, "If that generation of believers will 'die' like Enoch (which we know isn't a death at all), don't you think they might live like him also?" In other words, the believers who are alive when Jesus returns will already be reaching for and finding the eternal realms of Heaven. Just like Enoch, they will wander closer and closer to the dimensional barrier until it seems more appropriate to be *there* instead of here. So when Jesus comes, He will gather to Himself a generation of people who are already familiar with the heavenly dimension. They will have already started seeing it, feeling it, and living in it. It's even possible they could be visiting that dimension in their bodies, just like Enoch and Elijah, before they enter in for good.

If you're doing the math, that makes 3 Enoch like moments for humanity (we're still not counting Jesus' translation because it is a bit different): First Enoch, then Elijah, and finally, everyone who is "in Christ" at the end of this age. And it's also interesting that there is one Enoch moment per age. Enoch lived in the age of Taurus. Elijah in the age of Aries. And before the age of Pisces comes to an end, I believe we will see a great number of Enochs awaiting Jesus' coming.

Now back to our original question. Where is our pursuit of the heavenly dimension taking us? It's leading us to a familiarity with the other realm that is so complete we can go there in our bodies as well as in the Spirit. In short, it's leading us to an Enoch like translation. Sound crazy? Just remember that this mass translation has already been prophesied in the scriptures. Also, take into account when it occurs. It happens at the transition between the age of Pisces and Aquarius, which is the moment of Jesus' return, which just happens to be the very moment in time we are about to experience. In light of all of this, I believe our movement towards the heavenly dimension, which we see growing with each passing day, is none other than the birthing of the Enoch generation. Or, using our other term, I could call it the birthing of the transitionaries.

The Enochs (the transitionaries) will probably be the very first picture the world will see of the life of the next age, which is first and foremost an age for immortals – for people who have finished the story of restoration. And it's okay for that birthing to take some time. No matter how humble your first efforts to reach into Heaven are, you should never stop going. Even if it is hard to break free from the pull of a fallen earth, each minute spent in the heavenly dimension brings you closer to an Enoch experience. If we need a bit more encouragement, consider Jesus' words about "letting go."

For whoever desires to save his life will lose it, but whoever loses his life for My sake will find it. (Matthew 16:25)

There is no doubt that letting go of a mortal life is a daunting affair, but don't give up. Keep reaching up to Heaven. Learn to live there. Finding your eternal life is the perfect introduction to the next age, which is none other than an age of immortal kingship.

Part 4:

Discovery

I suspect that, for the Church, it will not be easy. It will not be easy for the nursing mother to accept the possibility that her charge has grown to need additional nourishment; or that revelation of the mystery of the kingdom was not turned off at the tap when the New Testament canon was closed, but is the work of an earth-time.

- Owen Barfield, Saving the Appearances

Therefore let us leave the elementary doctrine of Christ and go on to maturity ... And this we will do if God permits.

- Hebrews 6: 1-3

Chapter 12

A History of Discovery

Everyone that I know, myself included, who has devoted time and effort to experiencing Heaven in the Spirit, has come away with a few things in common: First, everyone seems to be struck by how good God is to them and how much He loves them. Second, everyone finds out that God is ready to share all kinds of new things with them. Any trip to Heaven is basically a voyage into the unknown, and while sections of the Bible like Revelation paint a very vivid picture of Heaven, I believe from my own experiences that there is so much more up there than what's already been written about in the scriptures.

"It will always behoove us to keep testing and analyzing our experiences, even if that means we have to take our time."

Therefore, you are bound to come across something no one has ever seen before. Years into my own heavenly journeys, sitting in my heavenly library, I was reading a book about the heavenly signs (*Stars for All Seasons*). That book only exists in Heaven, and at least some of the information it contained was unprecedented in my experience. I have yet to find any mortal reference to the revelatory signs as I described them to you in previous chapters. Since I have been unable to cross reference that particular bit of heavenly wisdom, I am only left to wonder if an understanding of the revelatory sign of an age is a discovery of something new. At first, that was surprising and challenging. It provoked the question, "Are we allowed to see and hear things that haven't been seen and heard before?" In short, are we allowed to discover new things?

I wonder how many others have faced this issue of discovery, since the idea of visiting the heavenly realms has been around for about 6,000 years (consider Enoch again). I can only guess how many new and groundbreaking treasures have been seen and then forgotten, written about and then lost, or just kept quietly within by people over the last millennia? We may never know the entire breadth of their discoveries. Even the apostle Paul, when talking about his own heavenly experience, wouldn't divulge everything (2 Corinthians 12:4). Personally, I can see why it's tempting to just keep quiet about it. However, when we go through a major cosmic shift, the new and novel things seem to come out whether we like it or not. Therefore, the question, "Is discovery even allowed?" is probably going to be a significant one.

Another example of seeing something unprecedented came when I first started meeting the families of angels. The fourth angel I ever met was named Creedalynn, and there was no mistaking her feminine appearance. She had long dark hair. She appeared in an elaborate dress made of white and green and adorned with emeralds. She was a female angel. Now, if you were brought up in church like I was, you might have thought,

"Am I allowed to see female angels? Aren't they all supposed to be male?" I searched the scriptures for some passage for or against the existence of angelic women, and I didn't find anything that ruled it out. In fact, the Bible seemed curiously silent on the issue of angelic gender.

If I had come across a passage of scripture where the Lord said, "Thou salt not see any female angels," then I would surely have done some serious "testing of the spirits" and prayed about it until I stopped seeing female angels or the Lord revealed them for what they really were. The point being, if the scriptures said explicitly not to do something, then I'm not going to do it. There are plenty of reasons to keep the scriptures at the forefront of your experiences in the Spirit. No one is perfect, and all of our experiences should be tested and approved by the Bible to make sure our heavenly journeys stay safe and truthful.

Just because we've been given an enormous freedom to explore the heavenly realm does not mean we should stop using common sense to filter out those things that are clearly out of line with God's character and instructions. Just for the record, if an angel I meet in Heaven tells me to go rob a bank, I'm not listening. I will simply back out of the experience and go spend some time with my heavenly Dad. I don't need to listen to a spirit say something to me in direct conflict with the words of my Father, "Do not steal."

However, if the scriptures aren't in opposition to something, does that give us the go ahead to peer into something unknown? Can we cautiously keep moving forward with the new insight? I use the word "cautiously" here on purpose. It will always behoove us to keep testing and analyzing our experiences, even if that means we have to take our time. In the end, the responsibility will be on the person visiting Heaven in the Spirit. It will be his or her job to constantly test anything new with these basic principles: Does it contradict God's character and plan as He has given in the scriptures? And, does it bring you closer to your heavenly Father? Another way to look at this is whether or not your heavenly travels have caused the fruit of the Spirit to increase in your life (Galatians 5: 22-23). If not, then no matter what cool thing you have found in your heavenly experiences, it's time to ask the hard question of how involved the Holy Spirit has been in your journeys.

"If I could sum up the fundamental difference between the Israelites listening to Moses' claims, and the bulk of Christians today, it would be this: Those Israelites did not believe they knew everything there was to know about God and His kingdom! But for some reason we think we do know all there is to know."

Now that that very important disclaimer is out of the way, we can look more seriously at my question about female angels. The Bible didn't say that all angels were male; in fact, it said nothing definitive about the gender of angels. Furthermore, Jesus didn't seem bothered at all by the notion, so I decided to keep going. Over the course of years I found these angelic women to be as important, helpful, and precious as any of the angelic men I had met. And I did eventually find a reference in the Bible that does seem to validate their existence. You can find it in the book, Zechariah.

> *Then the angel who talked with me came out and said to me, "Lift your eyes now, and see what this is that goes forth." So I asked, "What is it?" And he said, "It is a basket that is going forth."*
> *Then I raised my eyes and looked, and there were two women, coming with the wind in their wings; for they had wings like the wings of a stork, and they lifted up the basket between earth and Heaven. (Zechariah 5: 5 – 10)*

I chuckled to myself when I saw this, because it does appear to be a reference to two female angels. I had spent quite some time getting up the courage to say I believed in female angels, and as it turned out I shouldn't have been so worried. However, the whole experience taught me some valuable lessons about discovery – even though I'm not sure this experience counts anymore as an actual discovery of something unprecedented.

My conflict with the existence of female angels was really a struggle with the nature of the canonized Bible. Even though, as we've just seen, the Bible might actually confirm the presence of angelic women, I was unaware of it, and that made it feel a little dangerous to me. It felt that way because over the course of my Christian life, I had been taught that the Bible contained everything God ever wanted me to know. So if it wasn't in the canonized Bible, I didn't need to know it. The problem of course came when I started visiting Heaven and finding out things that didn't necessarily have a reference point in scripture. In order to keep going on my heavenly journeys (and I think this will happen for anyone else who makes the same commitment to the unseen things), I had to ask myself some hard questions about the Bible and what it has to say about discovery. The relationship between those two (the Bible and discovery) is a veritable minefield. In order to tiptoe through the mines without causing unneeded injury, let's take a quick look at spiritual discovery in history.

One of my favorite discoverers is Moses, primarily because his discovery was so grand and yet the significance of it is often lost on us – and I'm not talking about the law (Torah), either. Maybe more important than receiving the Torah on Mt. Sinai is what happened before they all left Egypt, when Moses was just getting started in his role as deliverer. The spirit of adventure and discovery was all over him in those days. When he sees a burning bush, he doesn't run, he looks closer. Then, during his encounter with the Almighty, his inquisitiveness takes over and he asks for God's proper name. And that could be the greatest discovery of Moses' life! God told him His first, proper name, and that had never been known before!

Now, I want you to imagine being in the Israelite camp in Egypt and hearing Moses speak for the first time. I want you to imagine a man claiming to be sent by the God of Abraham, Isaac, and Jacob, and then filling in the specifics about God that those aforementioned forefathers didn't even know. Would you have believed him? If someone claimed to know God's first name, and no one in your culture had ever known it, would you buy it? I'm sure the miraculous signs helped to convince the people that Moses was sent by God, but I'm amazed at how readily the Israelites accepted something completely new.

"Almost all of the advice that Paul gives to the budding gentile churches had no reference point in the former age."

For the sake of comparison, imagine someone standing up in church and claiming to know God's middle name! Miraculous signs or not, I think we would have a very big problem receiving such a message for the same reasons I mentioned earlier – we have an ingrained aversion to something new and Biblically unprecedented. I can imagine someone accosting the speaker and saying, "If God wanted us to know His middle name, He would have put it in the Bible!" Amazing how much things have changed over the millennia, for no one in Moses' hearing said, "If God wanted us to know His first name, He would have told Abraham!" The simple fact is that the Israelites of Moses' day did not think they knew everything there was to know about God. In fact, it was very clear to them that they had much more discovery to go through before their story was over. They were enslaved in Egypt, and that was not the fulfillment of God's promises to their forefathers. Therefore, they expected to find out more about God and His plan. Discovery wasn't just allowed or tolerated, it was hoped for!

If I could sum up the fundamental difference between the Israelites listening to Moses' claims, and the bulk of Christians today, it would be this: Those Israelites did not believe they knew everything there was to know about God and His kingdom! But for some reason (vanity? deception? ignorance?) we think we do know all there is to know. So when did it change? When did we stop hoping for new discoveries and embracing the unprecedented? Certainly, we can still see the fires of discovery burning with Jesus, His followers, and the Apostle Paul. I've mentioned in previous chapters how much courage and boldness it took to leave behind the spiritual commission and practices of the age of Aries and embrace the blank slate of the age of Pisces. Remember all the discussion about new commissions, new ways to worship, and new titles and offices? Almost all of the advice that Paul gives to the budding gentile churches had no reference point in the former age. The apostle was revealing the practices and methods of the new age as quickly as he got them. Discovery indeed!

> *"God was expected to say things that no one had ever heard or written down before."*

If discovery was still accepted at the beginning of this age, what happened afterwards to make it so scary? (Read carefully here, because we are about to enter the minefield!) I believe it all changed when the Biblical canon was closed. Prior to the canonization, Israel had a constantly evolving cache of scripture. There were books around at the time of Jesus and Paul that had only been written just a few centuries prior. Daniel, all of the minor prophets, the book of Enoch, and the apocryphal writings were all relatively recent additions, but were accepted as inspired and holy by believers in the first century A.D. They expected to be taught, that the revelation of the Kingdom of God was a work in progress, and that as writings came about that were clearly divinely inspired, they should be accepted as such. In other words, the accepted "canon" of scripture was not closed.

Then, about 3 or 4 centuries after the advent of Christianity, the powers that be decided to create a closed canon of scripture so that nothing else could be considered as inspired or holy. Just to reiterate, for thousands of years God had been revealing things about Himself and His kingdom, and as He revealed them, chosen people wrote those things down. There is no period of Israel's history when someone wasn't writing something inspired – even in the darkest of times. And then, as if someone flicked a switch, a decision was made to put a bookend on those writings, effectively ending the period of authoritative revelation. Let's not forget that the people who did this were trying to protect Christendom from false gospels and solidify what Christianity was all about, so we can at least see why closing the canon seemed like a good idea to them. However, the negative effect that had on discovering new things is still very much with us today.

When the decision was made to put a bookend after John's Revelation, the message was clear – no more discovery allowed. From that point on, you were only allowed to believe what the saints who lived many years before you believed. You could only trust the revelations of the past. Nothing new. I'd like to point out that even today, as much as 1,600 years after the canon was closed, almost every sermon heard in a church begins with the phrase, "Open your Bible to..." With extremely rare exceptions, all sermonizing is a review of past revelations at least 2,000 years old. Only a daring preacher might start with the statement, "You can keep your Bibles closed today, because I have never seen nor heard before what I'm about to tell you."

While that would seem borderline heretical to us (certainly untrustworthy), that was the exact position of people like Isaiah, Jesus, and Paul, to name a few. They all quote and reference revelations that were still very recent, nor did they shy away from saying something that no one had ever heard before. For them, the revelation of God and His kingdom was an ongoing process. God was expected to say things that no one had ever heard or written down before. Therefore, I believe we must see the Bible as a divinely inspired, sacred, and a Holy narrative that is still revealing itself. God has not stopped speaking to us! That story did not stop progressing when the writers of the New Testament all died out, but that is often what we think. And again, I can sympathize with the bishops who closed the canon, because protecting Christianity from false gospels is a serious task! And, as I will explain later, none of this – in any way – diminishes the role of the scriptures. But now I believe it's time to consider that a closed Bible (a closed revelation) is not exactly Biblical!

"The very Bible itself, with all its authority, points towards more discovery. If our future state "hasn't yet been revealed," then it's fair to say that we don't know the whole story."

For anyone who appreciates the cold, hard facts of the matter, consider this: A closed canon of scripture was never prophesied. Jesus never commanded it, nor did any Old Testament prophet or New Testament Apostle. There simply isn't a scripture that even alludes to the period of authoritative revelation coming to a close (some may point to the the last lines of John's Revelation as the reason for closing the cannon, but it is an enormous reach to think of that warning as applying to the collection of sacred writings known as the Bible – which didn't even exist at the time Revelation was written). So if this idea isn't in the Bible itself, then it must be in some other category. Most of us would call a regulation that has no prior precedent in the scriptures simply a religious tradition. In the long run, perhaps a few hundred years from now, the closing of scripture might be considered the deepest rooted religious tradition of the age of Pisces. I'm not sure how we can call it anything else. But let's tread carefully here. Anytime we are dealing with a tradition, especially a religious one, suggesting a different view of things can invite some extreme criticism.

To any potential critics, please keep in mind these disclaimers: I believe that every one of the 66 books of the Bible is completely inspired and holy. I cherish every one of those books and will always defend their value. Personally, I view the closing of the canon, and the books that make up the canon to be completely different issues. The books themselves are priceless. They are the very words of God. On the other hand, the canonization of those books was a decision made by human men to clarify what was authoritative revelation. That, in and of itself, is still a good thing. But closing the canon, despite all the good reasons for doing it, implied that God was done telling the story of Himself and Man. That assumption is in direct conflict with the very scriptures being canonized. For instance:

Beloved, now we are children of God; and it has not yet been revealed what we shall be, but we know that when He is revealed, we shall be like Him, for we shall see Him as He is. (1 John 3: 2)

We cannot put on blinders and pretend we didn't read this verse in 1 John 3:2. The very Bible itself, with all its authority, points towards more discovery. If our future state "hasn't yet been revealed," then it's fair to say that we don't know the whole story. Sooner or later there will be voices proclaiming those things that John had not seen.

"... the Bible, itself, is a history of discoveries. Each book is a new piece of the puzzle. Each volume is there solely because its author found out something new about God."

Once the Bible had a "last book", religious life as a whole took on a fear of going outside of the canonized Bible. Discovery was considered to be synonymous with deception. There's even a scripture verse commonly taken way out of context to reinforce this fear (1 Corinthians 4:6). In that passage, Paul is encouraging the Corinthians not to infer more from his letter than what he wrote, but it is often used as a proof to keep folks from looking for more revelation. People like to quote Paul and say, "Don't go beyond what is written." However, I find it hard to imagine Paul telling people to "not go beyond what is written" when that was the very essence of his own ministry! On the other hand, there is a very good reason for this fear. We are not unopposed in this world, for there are plenty of wicked spiritual forces that want to get us off track. Deception is a very real tool in the Devil's arsenal, and for that reason alone, we should look at anything extra-biblical with a wary eye. The road between a fear of discovery and false discovery (deception) is a narrow one.

It's here, on the narrow road of discovery, that the canonized Bible is of enormous value. It gives us the standards and foundations of God's character, His plan, and how He reveals Himself. It is the ultimate reference point for any further understanding, and disregarding it in any way is inviting catastrophe. And lest we miss it, the Bible, itself, is a history of discoveries. Each book is a new piece of the puzzle. Each volume is there solely because its author found out something new about God. Let's consider again those words from 1 John, chapter 3.

...and it has not yet been revealed...

Sooner or later, the bookend that was placed after John's Revelation will be removed, and what was previously unknown will be revealed. I hope it isn't surprising to us, because God has been doing this from the very beginning. Only our religious traditions will keep us from accepting the rest of the story. In my opinion, that is as dangerous a trap as any other deception. And one that the devil would gladly use to keep God's people out of the heavenly realms, thus inhibiting the fulfillment of God's will in the coming age.

Chapter 13

Heresy and Orthodoxy

There's something very satisfying about having God and His ways all figured out. Of course, I'm not sure that's ever possible, but it's something we like to believe because it takes the risk out of eternity. Let me explain what I mean. If you know you need a lot of help to get out of the fallen state you are in, and if you know that God has a plan to get you out, then you probably want to know exactly what the Lord has to say about you and that plan. If there are any unknowns in that relationship, there will always be a fear that something very important has been missed. We definitely don't want any curve balls thrown at us, because that would introduce the fear that we don't have it all figured out yet. And if we don't have it all figured out, then are we as safe and eternally secure as we thought? You can see why we like our understandings of God to be static and unchanging.

> *"With the exception of the 12 who would follow Him no matter what the risks, the rest of the masses just couldn't handle the idea that God would change something that they had known for so long."*

Change involving God feels downright dangerous. So when it comes to something like our eternal salvation or the beliefs that can assure it, we like to keep around a list of beliefs that are without error. Only the beliefs that everyone can agree are safe and will keep you out of hell make these lists. The fancy word for this is orthodox beliefs. When you read the Nicene Creed or the Apostles Creed, you are seeing an example of orthodoxy. Those creeds are the statements of faith that are trusted and foundational, and they're there so that we all know what we need to believe in order to get it right with God. Stray from that list, and you find yourself on another list called heresy. Heresies are the beliefs that are contrary to the orthodox beliefs, or at least they don't conform to the accepted orthodox traditions.

Now before we go into the relationship between these two paths, let's make another quick disclaimer – orthodoxy is a good thing. Just like the canonized Bible, orthodoxy is very helpful in avoiding deception. We know that if you keep to the list, like the Apostles Creed, you can't go wrong with God. Every one of us has needed that simple assurance at least once in our lives. So no matter what I'm about to say, please keep in mind this is not about throwing stones at one side or the other. It's about addressing the issue of discovery, and it's about finding out what that has to do with a change in the cosmic ages. As you can probably guess, this will not be a case of one side being "right" and the other "wrong." In fact, the relationship between orthodoxy and heresy is a complicated one, and it's hardly black and white.

Let's look at a moment in Jesus' ministry when He took His disciples down the path of discovery and forced them to consider the no man's land between orthodoxy and heresy. We can find it in the gospel of John, right after He miraculously fed the 5,000.

Then Jesus said to them, "Most assuredly, I say to you, unless you eat the flesh of the Son of Man and drink His blood, you have no life in you. Whoever eats My flesh and drinks My blood has eternal life, and I will raise him up at the last day. For My flesh is food indeed, and My blood is drink indeed. He who eats My flesh and drinks My blood abides in Me, and I in him. As the living Father sent Me, and I live because of the Father, so he who feeds on Me will live because of Me. This is the bread which came down from Heaven - not as your fathers ate the manna, and are dead. He who eats this bread will live forever." (John 6: 53 – 58)

From that time many of His disciples went back and walked with Him no more. Then Jesus said to the twelve, "Do you also want to go away?" But Simon Peter answered Him, "Lord, to whom shall we go? You have the words of eternal life. Also we have come to believe and know that You are the Christ, the Son of the living God." (John 6: 66 – 69)

Eating Jesus' flesh and drinking His blood sounds strange no matter how you say it, so we tend to forgive the people who left Him that day. A closer look, though, might reveal just what happened in that fateful moment. Keep in mind that this conversation with His disciples comes right on the heels of a massive miracle (feeding the 5000) that resulted in many proclaiming Him to be "the Prophet that has come into the world."

Whatever occurred in this conversation was enough to put off the people who had seen one of the most otherworldly and undeniable demonstrations of God's power to date (there's a reason why the miraculous feeding is included in every gospel). It must have taken something really negative to outweigh the amazing thing they had just witnessed. What could make that many people decide – in an instant – that Jesus couldn't be trusted? I think it was more than just Jesus saying something strange that made them a little uneasy. I think He committed heresy.

First, consider Jesus' audience. They were all Jews and well versed in the law. Now, take a look at one specific commandment that Jesus may have challenged that day:

> *Moreover you shall not eat any blood in any of your dwellings, whether of bird or beast. Whoever eats any blood, that person shall be cut off from the people.'" (Leviticus 7: 26 – 27)*

Can you imagine what you might have felt that day? Here you are, following a man who can do things no one else can do. He is clearly sent from God. And then He says something that seemingly goes against the very law He is claiming to uphold and fulfill! What was a devout Jew to do in this scenario? To follow Jesus, in this case, meant departing from a well known precept in the Mosaic law.

Regardless of how metaphoric or symbolic the act of drinking His blood was thought to be, it was still way too close to error for a people who had been told for over a millennia, "Don't drink the blood!" The only reason the crowd of disciples would have left him that day, to "follow Him no more," was if He said something that pushed them too far. Recall that they believed He was sent from God. They believed He was the promised Messiah. But all of that changed when He challenged their orthodox understanding of God.

"... orthodoxy is a powerful tool in keeping us on the right path, but a very strong restrainer when it's time to embrace something new about God."

Remember why orthodoxy feels so good? It takes the risk out of our eternal salvation. It provides us with a deception free and error free code of belief. It's secure. However, in this moment, Jesus challenged that security. With the exception of the 12 who would follow Him no matter what the risks, the rest of the masses just couldn't handle the idea that God would change something that they had known for so long. They might have thought, "What if drinking His blood causes us to fall out of favor with God? What if it puts us at risk of God's displeasure and possibly hell?" Now contrast that with our attitude about the same issue, some 2,000 years later. We take the safety of these beliefs completely for granted, but for the people who first heard them, it was just too dangerous. What if this one statement knocked them off the path of orthodoxy and into the doubtful and uncertain sea of heresy?

The issue of drinking His blood was not the only heresy

Jesus would proclaim. Over and over again, Jesus refers to God as His Father. I know, that really doesn't sound like a big deal does it? But what we don't take into account in our modern understanding is that, prior to Jesus, no one related to God as a personal father. If you look for references to God as a "Father" in the Old Testament, you will only find about a dozen references to God as the Father of the nation, Israel. It was a generic way of saying that God founded the nation. Isaiah 9:6 is a good example of this. While there are many names of God recorded in the Old Testament, none of them involve the incredibly personal name for "Father" that Jesus uses when He talks about the Almighty. As many linguists have uncovered, the word Jesus uses for "Father" is anything but formal. It is a familiar term, much like our common word, "Daddy."

The identity of the Lord God as "Daddy" was as big a change from orthodoxy as anything we've considered. Just like the issue of drinking Jesus' blood, we've had 2,000 years to get used to this idea; but to the people who first heard it, it was unprecedented. Remember in the last chapter we spoke about Moses learning God's first name? Remember what an enormous moment of discovery that was in the history of the faith? This is the same kind of moment, only now, the God called YHWH (the name of God told to Moses) was known as a "Daddy".

"We take it for granted today that Jesus changed the very identity of God."

Jesus doesn't stop there. Just a few chapters into the first gospel, Matthew, Jesus is called the Son of God. And by the end of His ministry, Jesus commands His followers to baptize in the name of the Father, the Son, and the Holy Spirit. This trinity of persons is what we all believe today as the 3 parts of the Godhead. But to the Jews He was speaking to, it must have sounded like a completely different deity.

It's true that the Jews had a concept of God as a plural being. As early on as Genesis, God says, "Let us make man in our image." So we can be certain they thought the God-head had more than one aspect. However, the identity of those parts as a Father and Son (and later the Spirit) was a departure from orthodoxy of the highest order! It's a little too easy to say, "Shame on you Jews for not believing Jesus was the Messiah," when we realize what a leap of faith it would have taken to leave the orthodox beliefs and follow Him into the unknown. We might ask ourselves if we could have embraced such a drastic change. Again, orthodoxy is a powerful tool in keeping us on the right path, but a very strong restrainer when it's time to embrace something new about God.

When you read something as simple as Jesus teaching His disciples how to pray, you can see how He pushed them into uncharted waters at every turn. He tells them to start their prayer with, "Our Father." We struggle to imagine a world where people don't relate to God as a heavenly Father, but that is the exact world Jesus was born into. We take it for granted today that Jesus changed the very identity of God. He changed how God was known. He changed the names He was called by. Imagine something like this happening today and you can get a feel for the magnitude of Jesus' revelations. Maybe this sheds a little light on why Jesus and His followers were so persecuted by the religious establishment of their day. It's one thing to challenge the popular understanding of the law (Don't drink the blood); it's entirely another thing to change the orthodox understanding of who God is.

*Note: Even to this day, many Jews believe that Christians worship a different God than they do. The picture of God that Jesus painted for us (with a Father, a Son, and a Holy Spirit) was just too far outside the orthodox beliefs to even be considered the same deity. We should keep this in mind going forward.)

"... we can never take for granted that the things we believe to be at the very center of orthodox Christianity were absolute heresies to both Jew and Gentile when they were first spoken."

Jesus was a heretic, plain and simple. He was so unorthodox that His followers were still being persecuted by Jews and pagans for centuries after His death and resurrection! However, it's what happens when the persecution dies down that brings us to the point of this chapter. Within 4 centuries or so after Jesus' earthly ministry, all those crazy things He said had time to seep into the world, and before anyone might have noticed, those things weren't so crazy anymore. For much of the world, Christianity was becoming normal, and all of the new doctrines and beliefs were considered to be true and unerring. In fact, it's those very beliefs about Jesus' blood (taking Holy

Communion) and the nature of the Trinity that made up some of the orthodox statements of faith that we already mentioned. Within 400 years or so after Christ, Heresy had become Orthodoxy.

Now going forward we cannot say, "Once a heresy, always a heresy." And we can never take for granted that the things we believe to be at the very center of orthodox Christianity were absolute heresies to both Jew and Gentile when they were first spoken. With this in mind, we should start thinking about future heresies – the things that God is about to reveal that will challenge the things we already know. This has happened before, and it is sure to happen again.

Chapter 14

Courageous Transitions

Before we go any further, let's do a quick recap of what we've covered in the last few chapters. The first chapter of this section, "A History of Discovery," is there to deal with one of the problems we face when God tells us something that was previously unknown. We discussed how the closed canon of scripture has given us the sense that God is done telling the story, and that anything worth knowing has already been said by believers living 2,000 years ago. My hope is that you walked away from that chapter with a different view – that the Bible clearly points to more authoritative discovery, and that it cannot possibly contain the entire story. The disclaimers of that chapter are all about affirming the authority of the scriptures in the light of that different view.

The previous chapter, "Heresy and Orthodoxy," is all about the nature of new discoveries and how they are received over time. Initially, we saw how unprecedented truth is often completely rejected by the status quo. Then it eventually becomes orthodox tradition, and everyone seems to forget that it sounded like total lunacy just a little while before. I'm hoping we don't take for granted that we effortlessly believe things that required great leaps of faith from the good, orthodox minded people who first heard them.

Perhaps the most important thing I hope you take from the last chapter is that even such enormously important things like God's identity are not static. That doesn't mean God is changing who He is; it just shows us that our understanding of Him is not complete, and there is still more to experience. If we can reckon with this – that God introduces new parts of His person from age to age – then we will be a long way down the road to discovery.

Now we need to put a few pieces of the puzzle together, and to do that we need to recall some information about the cosmic ages. If you remember, Abraham and Jesus were both transitionaries who led the way into a new age. Both of them revealed a new commission, new practices, and as we just saw with Jesus, new beliefs about the nature of God. Abraham did this too, which is why He is called the "father of monotheism."

Overall, we get the picture that cosmic transitions are enormous spiritual upheavals. Today we stand at the precipice of another cosmic age. It only stands to reason that the same kind of spiritual shakeup is about to occur. Yes, it is very possible that within this next century (and my guess is much, *much* sooner), we will be introduced to ideas about God and His plan that are as revolutionary as the ones spoken by Jesus and His disciples. It's a lot to take in, but readying ourselves for things that seem out of this world is one of the primary focuses of this book. In a moment we are going to dive into some of those otherworldly things; but before we do, I'd like to make some concluding remarks about discovery.

Personally speaking, the only reason I have the confidence to proceed into the unknown is that I have experienced the love of God, and it overpowers my fears of being unsettled. Remember, at the beginning of the chapter, "A History of Discovery," I mentioned what everyone seems to find in their heavenly journeys? They discover that God loves them more. More than they thought or dreamed or believed. Something about that promised acceptance gives us the courage to set out on the sea of discovery, and maybe that's why it is what we all seem to find first.

"God has not reached the pinnacle of His awesomeness – nor will He. He will never find the ceiling of how great He is. Therefore, we will never find the ceiling of His greatness, either."

It could well be the case that none of us would continue visiting Heaven, with all of its unprecedented views, if we didn't have this confidence from the start. But once it does set in, we seem to take off into a world that is "abundantly beyond all that we ask or think" (Ephesians 3:20). Since God is always doing more than we can ask or think, we will always be stumbling into new things. I like to think of it this way: God has not reached the pinnacle of His awesomeness – nor will He. He will never find the ceiling of how great He is. Therefore, we will never find the ceiling of His greatness either. He will go on forever discovering new levels of His own glory, and we will happily try to keep up. We will go from "glory to glory" and from discovery to discovery. His always increasing love for us is the thing that keeps us settled in the midst of an eternally developing relationship.

Also, it's the thing that keeps us confident in the face of

certain errors. On this side of eternity, no one but Jesus is going to get it all right. We are sure to make a mistake here and there. If I'm wrong about female angels or the heavenly book *Stars For All Seasons*, I don't need to despair. I can still trust in God's love and acceptance more than my ability to get it all right.

In other words, once we have come face to face with how much we're loved, we aren't so afraid of failure. We know that, no matter what, God has a plan to fix every error, correct every bad assumption, and cover over any misinterpretation. Of course, the alternative to this is a fear of God that paralyzes us and keeps us from experiencing "abundantly beyond all that we ask or think." It's His love that showed us the "abundantly beyond" of the Kingdom in the first place. And it's His love that has already accounted for all of our shortcomings as we reach for it. That security is now my only rightful license to go forward and theorize about the cosmic changes on our horizon. Towards the end, I'll make some comments about testing our theories. When we get there, just remember that should our efforts to look ahead prove wrong (or even only partially understood or misunderstood) in some ways, we shouldn't lose heart. God has a wonderful plan. Let's just do our best while "we lean not on our own understanding" but trust God with *everything* (Proverbs 3:5-6).

At the moment, I have to label my thoughts about the next age as theories, no matter how much I am convinced of them, personally. A theory, in its root meaning, is a contemplation or speculation. What we need going forward (and I think this is true for spiritual meetings of any kind) is an environment that allows for some good spiritual speculation. The validity of those ideas will have to stand up to time. Only God's activity in the next age can affirm them or not. For now, all we need is an environment that is open to the question, "What will we learn about God's identity in the next age? What will be the big spiritual changes?"

One of my theories is that I think we are going to be reintroduced to the Holy Spirit. Even though we've known that the Holy Spirit is a part of the Godhead, I'm not sure we've grasped yet what the Spirit is. Or rather, *Who* the Spirit is. To me, that's a relationship I am eager to fully discover. However, it's not the only eternal relationship that interests me or that I believe God has new revelations about. I'm constantly asking the question, "If God made Adam and Eve to be together – and that was before mankind fell from perfection – won't He restore some kind of male and female romantic relationship when things are perfect again?" Our loving, romantic relationships are such a big part of human life. Naturally, many of us have wondered what eternity would be like with or without them. Before we're done, I'm going to throw in my ideas (and remember they are just that – ideas!) on that subject as well.

That is my roadmap going forward, and to some readers it may appear to be an odd choice of subjects. Let's recall, one more time, that when the ages change, the shifts almost always take us into brand new directions. Oftentimes, the conversations on the fringe of spiritual society end up being at the center of spiritual life in the arriving age. So what seems to be on the periphery of the age of Pisces might just be the center of orthodoxy in Aquarius. Ultimately, I'm highlighting these next age issues because they deal with our relationship with God, and our own identity. I believe everything else about the next age will be born out of that foundation.

Part 5:

The Eternal Relationships

Every heart sings a song,
incomplete, until another heart
whispers back. Those who wish
to sing always
find a song.

– Plato

Many waters cannot quench love,
Nor can the floods drown it
If a man would give for love
All the wealth of his house
It would be utterly despised.

– Song of Solomon 8:7

Chapter 15

Father and Mother

Ask someone to imagine the Holy Spirit, and you get a lot of different answers. To some, the Spirit takes the classical form of a dove. For others, the Spirit is more like animated water, taking on a vaguely human form. The Holy Spirit has been described as wispy, colorful, faint, mysterious, sometimes with form, and sometimes without. The underlying theme in all of these descriptions is that the Holy Spirit isn't well defined, and I think that is about to change. A friend of mine told me once that he never really related to the Holy Spirit as a distinct, stand alone, person. Rather, he always related to the Spirit as the spirit of the Father, or the spirit of Jesus. To him, the Holy Spirit was more like the spiritual stand in for the two more well known persons of the Godhead, almost like an extension of them. Given our most common examples of interacting with the Spirit, it would seem we expect this person to be a force directing our steps, providing supernatural power, and bringing helpful things to mind – not all that much different than our notion of an angel. Not many people will say with confidence that they really know Who the Holy Spirit is outside of that framework.

No matter what you've thought in the past or what your denominational preference is today, I'd like you to consider the following question logically and reasonably: A Holy Father has a Holy Son, so the natural remaining member of that relational trio is a _____. If you answered, Holy Uncle or Holy Pet Dove, you're not being honest with yourself. I have come to believe the only logical member left out of that picture is a mother. Now we just need to see if our sense of logic and common sense is supported by any evidence.

Our first clue would come from the original language of the Bible, Hebrew. Before we jump into the word for "Spirit" in the Bible, let's go over some facts about languages: First, many languages, including Hebrew, incorporate a gender for nouns. That means that some words are considered masculine and other words are considered feminine. Second, those languages that utilize gender in words also allow the verbs to agree with the gender. If you remember this, you have two ways to see the gender of a word. Lastly, there have been some good studies lately on the Hebrew origin of both the Old and New Testaments. Books like *Lost in Translation*, written by John Klein and Adam Spears, explain how Hebrew was the primary language of Jesus and all the New Testament authors. There are many, many Hebrew concepts in the New Testament that just don't translate well into Greek and other languages. These Hebrew figures of speech show us that the first language of the Bible had to have been Hebrew.

Don't take my word for this though; read those books (and many other scholarly works) for yourself. Just to recap, we know that Hebrew considers some words to be masculine or feminine, and we know that the whole Bible would have been spoken and written in this language, regardless of the translations throughout history.

Now back to the word for Spirit, which in Hebrew is Ruach. If you hadn't guessed already, Ruach is a feminine noun, and it's coupled with feminine verbs. Just to reiterate, in a language that utilizes gender, having a feminine verb implies that the subject is also feminine. The word for the Spirit of God is a feminine idea in every way. That might seem confusing because everyone seems to call the Holy Spirit, "he." However, a quick look at the history of Biblical translations might shed some light on how we got there. In Greek, the word for Spirit is gender neutral, so after the first round of major translations the idea of the Spirit became more of an "it" than a "she." Once the faith was Romanized, the official language of translation became Latin. Latin also has a word for Spirit, but it is masculine. So you can see how the idea of the Spirit migrated from feminine to neutral to masculine, and it has stayed the same ever since.

At this point, someone might think, "So what if it's a feminine word? What does that have to do with the actual identity of that part of the Godhead?" By itself, not a lot. Let's keep looking and see how Jesus talked about the Holy Spirit, and keep in mind that when He spoke the word "Spirit" it carried a different gender than it does to us today. To begin, we'll check out the passage in John, chapter 3: 1 – 7:

> There was a man of the Pharisees named Nicodemus, a ruler of the Jews. This man came to Jesus by night and said to Him, "Rabbi, we know that You are a teacher come from God; for no one can do these signs that You do unless God is with him." Jesus answered and said to him, "Most assuredly, I say to you, unless one is born again, he cannot see the kingdom of God."

Nicodemus said to Him, "How can a man be born when he is old? Can he enter a second time into his mother's womb and be born?"

Now before we go any further, consider the words in this conversation. Jesus answers Nicodemus' question with a statement about being born again. We take this phrase entirely for granted; and yet birth (in any context) is a feminine issue. No *man* can give birth. Nicodemus' response to that is totally understandable; he just wants to know how he can be reborn from his mother's womb. Here's where it gets interesting. Once Nicodemus mentions a mother, Jesus reveals something big in the very next line:

Jesus answered, "Most assuredly, I say to you, unless one is born of water and the Spirit, he cannot enter the kingdom of God. That which is born of the flesh is flesh, and that which is born of the Spirit is spirit. Do not marvel that I said to you, 'You must be born again.' (John 3: 8)

Notice that Jesus says we have to be born twice. Once by the water and once by the Spirit. The birthing through water is the first, mortal birth by an earthly mother. The whole process of a mother's water breaking before delivery is a good way to see how we have been "born of water" first. Then the second birth is by the Spirit, and that's the birth that lets us see the kingdom of God. Just in case you missed it, who is doing the birthing when we are born again? The Spirit is! Now add into this conversation that Jesus' word for Spirit, in Hebrew, was a feminine noun, and we have a feminine subject doing a very feminine job – giving birth to us. This is the first time that Jesus says the word "Spirit" in the gospel of John; and it comes right on the heels of someone asking about the mother's womb. Therefore, if we are going to start looking for the identity of the Holy Spirit, we have to start considering the title of Mother. Let's recall that the Holy Spirit also plays a very similar role in the life of Mary, the mother of Jesus:

> *And behold, you will conceive in your womb and bring forth a Son, and shall call His name Jesus. Then Mary said to the angel, "How can this be, since I do not know a man?"*
> *And the angel answered and said to her, "The Holy Spirit will come upon you, and the power of the Highest will overshadow you." (Luke 1: 31, 34 – 35)*

Again, it's the work of the Holy Spirit along with the "power of the Highest" that allows Mary to gestate and deliver the Son of God. Could it be that we are seeing the Holy Spirit empowering Mary as a mother because that's what the Holy Spirit really is?

We could also look at the other descriptions of the Spirit as the Helper and Comforter, but I think you can ponder the feminine suggestions of those names on your own. Instead, I'd like to extrapolate a little and interpret the blessing of Pentecost in the light of this theory. If you remember, the Holy Spirit descended on the believers in Acts, chapter 2, on the day of Pentecost.

From that moment on, the New Testament writers coin

the phrase, "in the Spirit." It's used over 40 times after Pentecost, and it might be another clue for us. If we are to be born again by the Spirit, only this time instead of natural waters we are born out of heavenly waters, is it possible the phrase "in the Spirit" could be interpreted "in the womb?" Think about this with me. Nicodemus' original question was about entering into a womb, and Jesus points to the Spirit as that womb. Since there are plenty of references in the New Testament of the Holy Spirit being like water, thinking of the Holy Spirit as a heavenly water filled womb doesn't seem that far off.

"All this time we've been gestating, waiting for the moment of birth when we will come out of the heavenly womb with an incorruptible and perfect body. In other words, we were born once in a fallen state, but we are about to be born again in a resurrected state."

A Hebraic perspective of birth is not just the moment a baby is delivered; it's also the moment of conception. To be "born" is to be conceived, because that is the first moment your spirit puts on its first cells of flesh. With this understanding, consider that when you came to faith in Jesus, you were born again – conceived again – in the Spirit. From the time that faith in the Messiah has been an option (the last 2,000 years or so), people have trusted in Him and have been conceived anew. All this time we've been gestating, waiting for the moment of birth when we will come out of the heavenly womb with an incorruptible and perfect body. In other words, we were born once in a fallen state, but we are about to be born again in a resurrected state. What other place can we be except in our Mother's womb, awaiting that moment?

Consider that Jesus talked about the "birth pains" coming before His return and our ensuing resurrection to glorified bodies. Or how about the passage in Romans that speaks of "creation moaning and groaning and waiting for the sons of God to be revealed"? In all of these, the picture is of us being "in the Spirit" (inside our Mother), waiting to come out at the end of the age. To paint the picture even clearer, imagine a baby inside the womb and there are some direct parallels to our current state. A baby in utero can hear the voice and movements of its mother. It can feel her. It can also hear what's going on around her, and by default, that baby is with the mother wherever she goes. So it is with all those "in the Spirit." We hear the Spirit's voice. We go where the Spirit goes. Also, we can hear the voice of the Father speak to us as though His lips were pressed to the Mother's belly. Just like Paul mentioned, we don't yet hear these voices clearly. We hear "in part." Just as a baby is in the womb, the voices we hear are a little muffled and muted. We want to hear, but our ears aren't quite completely formed.

The same is true for our eyes. The moment of birth is the first moment when a newborn baby can see its mother. Up until that time, it just feels the mother from within. But when the baby is finally ready to come out and open its eyes, the first thing it looks upon is its mother. I believe that when we are resurrected, which is to say, reborn, the first thing we will discover is that the Spirit who has been protecting and nourishing us is our Mother. We will finally be able to see the immortal, heavenly mother with immortal, heavenly eyes. And of course, Dad will be right there too, smiling in approval that His Sons and Daughters have finally come out of their preparation. It would seem like a perfect heavenly family.

Armed just with our common sense, let's examine the idea of a heavenly family and revisit what was said at the beginning of the chapter. If we have a Father and a Son, the only logical member who is missing is the Mother. Furthermore, that's the only way to produce any offspring. There isn't a family on earth that can produce a Son from two male parents. Yes, western culture is trying to circumvent that basis of life in the form of same sex marriages, but it simply isn't possible to get a child from two males. You have to have a male and a female– a mother and a father – to reproduce.

Why would we think that the Godhead is two male parts plus an offspring? In the same way, why would we think that Heaven is a single parent home, with the Father doing the masculine work and trying to stand in for the feminine role as well? God has designed life for us, and the most basic unit of relationship is a nuclear family made up of a dad, mom, and kids. If we just approached this logically, and in light of the scriptures we've discussed, it seems hard for me to imagine the Holy Spirit as anything other than a Holy Mother.

I mentioned in the last section the importance of an environment where people can ask some good, unorthodox questions and put forth some theories. Well, the belief in a male Holy Spirit is very ingrained, so suggesting otherwise will definitely be considered unorthodox. Take a look at John, chapter 14, and you'll see the sections of scripture that use the pronoun "He" for the Holy Spirit. For the record, the "He" is not in the Greek text. It's actually just the gender neutral pronoun I've mentioned before. Also, we still have to consider that the original language of the gospel of John is Hebrew, which uses a feminine word for Spirit. Whoever translated that passage just couldn't imagine a world in which the Holy Spirit wasn't male, and they ignored or refused the Hebrew notion that the word was feminine, so without apology they gave it a masculine pronoun. Again, that was their judgment; the masculine pronoun is not in the writing.

I confess that the more I looked into this issue, the more I wanted it to be the way I'm describing to you. So, yes, I'm biased, but for a good reason. Knowing God as a true Father has changed my life. I've found that's true for anyone who practices relating to Him as their Dad. Consequently, if knowing God as your personal Father is such a blessing and leads to so many life altering changes, what could knowing a heavenly Mother do? I would think that looking up to Heaven and seeing not one, but two loving parents, who have the ability to conceive, birth, and raise children would be a huge leap forward in understanding our eternal adoption as sons and daughters. I don't know of another way to say it – it just seems proper.

For now, it can still be just a theory. We'll see if believers start to recognize a more feminine voice as we near the moment of birth, and we'll watch to see how the Holy Spirit looks to our immortal eyes – once we open them. For now, keep in mind that God is not threatened by logical, common sense speculation, especially if it has some scriptural support. In fact, I think that He (and possibly She) is excited we are asking the questions.

Chapter 16

The Image of Gender

There's an Old Testament name of God, El Shaddai, that translates as "The Many Breasted One," and Jesus spoke of wanting to gather His people "like a hen gathers her chicks," so it's not unusual to think of the Almighty expressing feminine characteristics. However, our traditional notion has always been of a male God playing a feminine role. Everyone agrees the feminine role is necessary, but we've relegated it to a function or personality trait of the Father. In other words, we've believed God can act out the feminine, as long as all God's parts stay masculine. To believe that part of God isn't just feminine, but an actual woman, is another leap that our orthodox traditions will label as wrong, wrong, wrong. Notice, though, that I'm not suggesting that God is only a woman, but rather that part of the Godhead is a woman. The other parts known as Father and Son are – and will always be – 100% male. So can part of God be a woman? We'll have to see what the history of discovery (the Bible) has to say about it.

To have a discussion about the gender of God as it relates to the Trinity, we'd better go back to the first moment in scripture when the concept of gender is introduced. It also helps when that introduction occurs right at the beginning of the story, when everything is still perfect. Here is the account of the creation of gender in Genesis. Let's look this over and see what we can learn about God's nature, as well as our own:

> Then God said, "Let Us make man in Our image, according to Our likeness; let them have dominion over the fish of the sea, over the birds of the air, and over the cattle, over all the earth and over every creeping thing that creeps on the earth." So God created man in His own image; in the image of God He created him; male and female He created them. Then God blessed them..."
> (Genesis 1: 26 – 28)

When God decides to make man in "Our image," the word choice is extremely important.

The word for "image" in Hebrew implies reflection. You could correctly read the passage this way, "Let Us make man in Our reflection." A Hebrew scholar (and friend) once told me that the connotation of "image" in this verse is like a perfect 3-D copy of the original, which brings on even more significance than being just the reflection of a mirror. So you could say the verse this way to really get the meaning, "Let Us make man as a perfect 3-D copy of ourselves." Regardless of any discussion about the Holy Spirit and God's gender, doesn't that make you consider your own creation a little differently? You were made to be a perfect copy of God! It's as if God looked in a mirror and traced what He (or she or *they*) saw, and out popped humanity.

Now let's focus on the actual gender God saw in the reflection. It was both male and female. So whenever you read this passage, you aren't just seeing the dual gender of humankind; you are seeing the gender of God's separate parts as well. In other words, part of God seems to be an actual woman in order for an actual woman to be seen in the reflection. Just to say it one more time, if God saw a "Him" and a "Her" in the reflection, that must mean that God is also equally a "Him" and a "Her." I hope we're starting to see why the notion of the Holy Spirit as a woman may not be that crazy after all.

"Personally, I can only imagine what it must be like for a woman to live in a faith that actively teaches that women are an afterthought to creation. In my opinion, this is far from the truth, and I'd like to see it change."

I'm going to take a slight detour here to address inequality among the sexes, especially as it pertains to the last age of Christian thought. If you grow up believing that God is all masculine, and that all 3 of His parts can be called "He," then what are you to think if you were born a woman? If only men are made in God's image, then whose image are women made in? Historically, it's been said that the woman was made from the man, and there is a scripture verse used to back that up:

For a man indeed ought not to cover his head, since he is the image and glory of God; but woman is the glory of man. For man is not from woman, but woman from man. Nor was man created for the woman, but woman for the man. (1 Corinthians 11: 7 – 9)

Think about that statement in the context of Genesis. Both man and woman were said to be a perfect 3-D copy of God. So, as far as identity is concerned, women are made in the image of God just as much as men. Whatever the above verse is trying to say, it can't be a revision of the creation story. To be clear, I don't think that's what the Apostle Paul was even getting at, and the rest of the verse makes that clearer:

For this reason the woman ought to have a symbol of authority on her head, because of the angels. Nevertheless, neither is man independent of woman, nor woman independent of man, in the Lord. For as woman came from man, even so man also comes through woman; but all things are from God. (1 Corinthians 11: 10 – 12)

It's unfortunate that the above passage isn't usually read through to its completion, because that's where we see that Paul is addressing an issue of authority and covering, and not commenting on which gender is more Godlike. All that talk about a head covering is pointing out that men and women are indeed different and fulfill different roles. That's a good thing, and I think those roles – with their differing areas of authority – should be reaffirmed.

Unfortunately for women, this has not been thought through, and instead, the verse is used to imply that women are some how lesser. That's because we misinterpret those different roles (authorities) as an inequality. Personally, I can only imagine what it must be like for a woman to live in a faith that actively teaches that women are an afterthought to creation. In my opinion, this is far from the truth, and I'd like to see it change. But, that change will have to involve an admission that part of God (I suspect in the form of the Holy Spirit) is as much a woman as the Father is a man.

On that note, there may be one more clue about gender that Jesus gives us when talking about the unpardonable sin. It's one of the most confusing (and terrifying) passages in the gospels; but when seen through the eyes of divine gender, it takes on a whole new meaning:

"Therefore I say to you, every sin and blasphemy will be forgiven men, but the blasphemy against the Spirit will not be forgiven men. Anyone who speaks a word against the Son of Man, it will be forgiven him; but whoever speaks against the Holy Spirit, it will not be forgiven him, either in this age or in the age to come. (Matthew 12: 31, 32)

If we think that there is the slightest chance Jesus identified the Holy Spirit as the Mother, then we can guess why He is so defensive of Her. Notice that it's okay to say whatever you want about Jesus – but nobody talks about Mom and gets away with it. Yes, even in those days, you don't talk about Mom unless you're trying to pick a fight. I believe this is yet another moment when Jesus shows us who He knows the Holy Spirit to be. Women are to be respected and defended if necessary, and it's not their job to fight on their behalves. That's what the sons are for. In this moment, I think we are seeing Jesus playing the part of the son perfectly, and observe that He throws in a mention of the "age to come," which just might be the age when the Holy Spirit is much more clearly known.

> "What many of us don't know is that the phrase "the cool of the day" (Genesis 3: 6 - 9, referring to God walking in the Garden of Eden) is formed from the one Hebrew word, "Ruach". If you remember, that's the word for Spirit, and it is simply a translation preference to render the meaning as "cool of the day." God was walking with the Spirit, Who is a person, not necessarily a time of day. I believe that paints a very interesting and intimate picture of the Father walking with the Mother in the garden..."

Let's review the identity of God through the ages. First, God is known as a plural being Who exists as the One Almighty God. Then it is revealed that the Messiah is the actual Son of God. After that, the Messiah shows that the other parts are personally knowable as Dad and the Holy Spirit. Now I believe we can perhaps theorize that the Holy Spirit is the Mother (given the hints from the Bible and the nudges from our common sense). I believe we can even dare to go further and suggest that the Spirit isn't just a feminine part of God that acts motherly, but rather an actual woman, since distinct and separate genders are part of God's perfect reflection. If this theory proves accurate, we are in for a drastic change in the way we communicate with God. Jesus did that sort of thing when He instructed us to pray "Our Father." It could be that in the next age a perfectly orthodox way to pray could begin with "Our Mother (or our Parents), who art in Heaven."

Not surprisingly, I think believers have felt this pull towards the Mother for quite some time, possibly millennia. For instance, Mary, the mother of Jesus, was an extraordinarily important figure in Catholic Christendom. Some have said her importance got excessive, and I'm inclined to agree with them – to a point. I pointed out in a previous chapter that Mary should be honored because of what the Bible says about her; but that's no excuse for any so called Mary worship that has gone on. However, I think the reason Mary has been a fixation to many believers is because she sparked that inward need for a mother, and people of faith grabbed onto that image with gusto. Could it be that the mother of Jesus is the closest thing we've seen – in the flesh – to the heavenly Mother, and that's why she's so revered?

To conclude, let's go back to the Garden of Eden. Right at the moment when mankind fell, we can see one more picture of the Godhead as a Father and Mother looking after their children:

So when the woman saw that the tree was good for food, that it was pleasant to the eyes, and a tree desirable to make one wise, she took of its fruit and ate. She also gave to her husband with her, and he ate. Then the eyes of both of them were opened, and they knew that they were naked; and they sewed fig leaves together and made themselves coverings.

*And they heard the sound of the Lord God walking in
the garden in the cool of the day, and Adam and his wife
hid themselves from the presence of the Lord God among
the trees of the garden. Then the Lord God called to Adam
and said to him, "Where are you?" (Genesis 3: 6 – 9)*

What many of us don't know is that the phrase "the
cool of the day," is formed from the Hebrew word, "Ruach".
If you remember, that's the word for Spirit, and it is simply a
translation preference to render it "cool of the day." But that
phrase just isn't in the text. Don't worry if you didn't know
that; it's an obscure piece of Hebrew knowledge for sure. It
was a friend of mine who revealed that to me after I taught
one evening about the Holy Spirit as the Mother. My friend
immediately connected the dots and realized that God was
walking with the Spirit, who is a person, not necessarily a
time of day. That paints a very interesting and intimate picture of the Father walking with the Mother in the garden, on
their way to check on the kids.

Also, observe the symmetry between the Lord and the
Spirit and Adam and his wife. All the characters in this story
are presented as couples. First we see what the Lord and His
wife (the Spirit) were doing, and then we see what Adam and
his wife were doing. Remember, Adam and his wife were a
perfect 3-D copy of God. I believe that their existence together as man and wife is only possible because the Godhead
enjoyed the same kind of relationship. Now it's time for us to
move on from the Mother and consider this original, natural
state of the first man and the first woman, which is none other than a holy romantic union.

Chapter 17

Eternal Romance

I'm sure you've heard the phrase, "They were made for each other." We use it all the time when we see a couple who are head over heels in love, or just so in tune to each other that their union seems to be the most natural thing ever witnessed. Well, if there was ever a couple that fits this phrase, it's Adam and his wife. They were, after all, literally made for each other. They are also the only people on record to exist before the fall of Man. So if we are going to try to extrapolate what it's like to live as incorruptible humans, and try to answer an age old question about romantic relationships in eternity, we have to look back to the introduction of Adam and Eve:

And the Lord God said, "It is not good that man should be alone; I will make him a helper comparable to him." Out of the ground the Lord God formed every beast of the field and every bird of the air, and brought them to Adam to see what he would call them. And whatever Adam called each living creature, that was its name. So Adam gave names to all cattle, to the birds of the air, and to every beast of the field. But for Adam there was not found a helper comparable to him. And the Lord God caused a deep sleep to fall on Adam, and he slept; and He took one of his ribs, and closed up the flesh in its place. Then the rib which the Lord God had taken from man He made into a woman, and He brought her to the man.

And Adam said: "This is now bone of my bones And flesh of my flesh; She shall be called Woman, Because she was taken out of Man." Therefore a man shall leave his father and mother and be joined to his wife, and they shall become one flesh. And they were both naked, the man and his wife, and were not ashamed. (Genesis 2: 18 – 25)

> *"... the role of companion and partner (for Adam) is so exclusive that even God could not, or would not, fulfill that role."*

Immediately after God created the Heavens and earth, and immediately after He proclaimed all of those things to be good, He found something that wasn't good – aloneness. So God made someone "comparable" to help Adam. The word for that companion has been translated as helpmeet, helper, and partner; and as we know, there was nothing else in the creation (outside of Adam) that could do this job. In order to give Adam true companionship, God made something from within Adam, not from without. This is an important shift. There was nothing on the earth that could be the perfect partner for Adam, and that included God. Notice what didn't happen in this scenario. God didn't look down and say, "Oh well, none of the animals will do as companions, so I guess I'll be Adam's partner instead." On the contrary, the role of companion and partner is so exclusive that even God could not – or would not – fullfill that role.

Then, to further the sacredness of the relationship between Adam and his wife, we have the verse about leaving one's father and mother to be joined together. That seems unremarkable to us; don't we all do this when we are married? However, notice that this verse occurs before anyone else had been born and then married off (yes, I'm taking a very literal approach to this), so the only father and mother that Adam could have left would have been the heavenly Father and Mother – his own Father and Mother. This is not to say that Adam was leaving God in any way. It's just establishing what relationship had the preeminence.

In the same way a man leaves the protective cradle of his parents to begin his own life, so was Adam leaving the bosom of God to begin life as a complete creation. Bear with me here. This may seem like a shock to some, but if you look at the facts of the matter, the most profoundly significant relationship in Adam's life was not just his relationship with God; it was also his relationship with his wife. This isn't much of a problem when we think it through, because the same is true for the Godhead, especially if you come to believe the Holy Spirit is our heavenly Mother. In this way, the relationship Adam had with his wife is the exact mirror image the Father had with the Mother. Then it seems perfectly natural that the foundation of mankind was two people, a man and a woman, in a completely exclusive and holy relationship.

*"All the joys that accompany that romance
– closeness, cooperation, affection, sex, and
inspiration – were engineered into the human
experience from the beginning. These things were
not products of the fall of mankind, they were
the products of perfection."*

If we needed one more proof for the parallel between Adam's wife and the Father's wife, consider that the name given to Adam's companion is awfully similar to the name for the Holy Spirit. They are both introduced as "helper."

And the Lord God said, "It is not good that man should be alone; I will make him a helper (Genesis 2: 18)

And I will pray the Father, and He will give you another Helper — the Spirit of truth (John 14: 16 – 17)

Could it be that this term, "helper," is the Biblical term for a man's female counterpart? Also, this term is hardly as simple as our modern notion of a helper – someone who makes it easier or provides some service. Linguists have done the work of interpreting this word, and it seems to imply a rich combination of all the different ways it's translated. Think of someone who is a partner, perfect companion, co laborer, and life giver, and you start to get the idea. The joining together of these two parts, the man and his wife, is presented in the first chapters of the Bible as the ultimate relationship. And in keeping with our theories, it is only this way because that is exactly what existed within God.

Now consider that when things were completely perfect, before the fall of mankind, the objective of God was to put a man and a woman together in a holy romantic relationship. We can call it "romantic" because it is an intimate, loving relationship between opposite genders. As we've already mentioned, it was the relationship that provided an end to all loneliness and incompleteness. It was provided to perfectly fulfill the desires of companionship. To me, this sounds very romantic. All the joys that accompany that romance – closeness, cooperation, affection, sex, and inspiration – were engineered into the human experience from the beginning. These things were not products of the fall of mankind. They were the products of perfection.

However, when you peruse the available Christian media, you might be convinced of the opposite. For instance, there is a lot of focus on experiencing a full and loving marriage while you're still on earth; but pick up a book about the afterlife and you get the picture that romance is just an earthly concern that will eventually pass away. In virtually every mainstream teaching about Heaven, the issue of male/female romantic relationships is either left out or completely denied.

It's as if we think these things are only important here, on a fallen earth, but once you get to Heaven you graduate from such mortal concerns. The dominant theory is that once you are perfected, you are just so close to God that you don't think about the loving union between a man and woman any more. Closeness to God is then presented as the "be all, end all" of human experience – as if the joy of that union trumps all others. That's a good theory, even if it isn't exactly true. We do need to be completely reconnected and restored to God – there's no denying that. But I think to say that unhindered relationship to God will fulfill every need and overpower basic human desires is missing the whole point of the Creation. In the beginning, while Adam enjoyed an unhindered connection to God, he still needed a "helper." He was still "alone" according to God.

It makes you wonder: Would God, Himself, purposefully create something (like an intimate relationship) that had no bearing whatsoever on anything in Eternity? If that were the case, why was the ancient Hebrew covenant of marriage so sacred? Could it be that God was continually pointing back to the perfect union of the Garden in the hopes of restoring that along with everything else lost in the fall of Man?

The concept of "no romantic relationships in eternity" is popular with Christian writers and teachers due to some verses in the gospel of Matthew. In fact, almost all of the "romanceless" teachings about Heaven are anchored on this verse. We're going to take a moment to deal with this passage because it gives us some insight straight from Jesus. I believe any alternate theory on this subject must consider His words very carefully.

The same day the Sadducees, who say there is no resurrection, came to Him and asked Him, saying: "Teacher, Moses said that if a man dies, having no children, his brother shall marry his wife and raise up offspring for his brother. Now there were with us seven brothers. The first died after he had married, and having no offspring, left his wife to

*his brother. Likewise the second also, and the third, even
to the seventh. Last of all the woman died also. Therefore,
in the resurrection, whose wife of the seven will she be? For
they all had her."*

*Jesus answered and said to them, "You are mistaken, not
knowing the Scriptures nor the power of God. For in the
resurrection they neither marry nor are given in marriage,
but are like angels of God in Heaven. (Matthew 22: 23
– 30)*

The Sadducees came to Jesus with an interesting thought experiment and His answer has been taken to affirm there are no romantic relationships in eternity. But some of that is based on our assumptions about what He said. We'll approach the issue of not being married or given away in marriage in a moment. First, let's deal with the assumptions about angels, since that's who Jesus said we will imitate.

Many people deduce that angels are genderless, or all male, or something totally unknown, and that they are incapable of the kind of relationships we would call romantic; but, surprisingly, the scriptures have something else to say on the matter. I've already discussed the issue of female angels in a previous chapter, but even if you don't buy into that just yet, you still have to reckon that all of the named angels in the Bible are presented as male. There isn't one reference in the Bible that suggests they are without gender or a combination of male and female together (hermaphroditic). So if we are to be like the angels in Heaven, that does not mean – in any way – that we will lose our gender. To believe otherwise is to assume something with no scriptural background at all!

Next, we have the assumption that angels are not capable of intimate relationships between genders. But take a look at this verse:

> *Now it came to pass, when men began to multiply on the face of the earth, and daughters were born to them, that the sons of God saw the daughters of men, that they were beautiful; and they took wives for themselves of all whom they chose. There were giants on the earth in those days, and also afterward, when the sons of God came in to the daughters of men and they bore children to them. Those were the mighty men who were of old, men of renown. (Genesis 6: 1 – 4)*

This is the classic passage about the Nephilim, and this subject is further explained in the book of Enoch and in 1 Peter. The gist of the story is that angels (translated as "sons of God" here and in other places) were falling from Heaven and marrying human women. The offspring they produced were giant human/angel hybrids called Nephilim, and this was the primary cause of the necessity of the Biblical flood, to eliminate these dangerous and unholy offspring.

"Paul's almost offhand reference (in 1 Corinthians 11:10) demonstrates that he was aware that angels could be attracted to women, and so he thought it very appropriate for a woman to display a symbol of her covering."

While that is certainly very interesting, what should stand out to us here is what this passage tells us about the angels. Fallen or not, angels must be able to appreciate physical beauty. Notice that these angels were attracted to human women. Also, we can't overlook that they were capable of intermarrying. That means angels must have the capacity for intimacy between the genders. And if we needed any more proof, we can see that these unions produced offspring, albeit unsanctioned and destructive offspring.

It's common for us to think that angels are so spiritual that they don't posses any noticeable gender or think about such "fleshly" issues as physical attraction. However, according to the Bible, they must be capable of both, which I think reinforces the idea that gender and attraction (one of the principles of romance) have been built into the foundations of all creation, not just humanity. Just take a look at nature and you can see the drama of male and female coming together in everything, whether it's the trees, animals, or even the opposite charges of electricity. And lest we think we're the only ones that noticed the angels possessing this quality, think about a quote from the Apostle Paul we looked at earlier:

For this reason the woman ought to have a symbol of authority on her head, because of the angels (1 Corinthians 11: 10)

Paul's almost offhand reference demonstrates that he was aware that angels could be attracted to women, and so he thought it very appropriate for a woman to display a symbol of her covering (a symbol of her protection). In Paul's day, that was an actual covering on her head. Also, if we look beyond these scriptural references and into the world of myths and legends, we can find many stories of angels, demigods, and other spiritual creatures doing the same kinds of things depicted in Genesis, chapter 6. And in all of those stories, the men are just as susceptible as the women to fall into relationships with these heavenly beings. There has always been a theme, in various cultures around the world, that heavenly beings could behave in ways that we think today are specifically human.

Let's take stock of where we are at this point. Jesus said that at the resurrection we would be like the angels in Heaven. So do angels have gender? There isn't any evidence to suggest they don't, while there are plenty of implications that they do. Personally, I think it's a safe bet that we will keep our gender after the resurrection. If there are separate genders, then is there attraction between them? Again, if we are going to be like the angels, then the answer is a resounding "yes".

Even though all the examples of human-like attractions we have of this are negative, they still reveal that angels notice beauty, experience attraction, and are capable of intimacy leading to reproduction. The bottom line is that Jesus' words are hardly limiting. The last thing any of this can imply is that eternity is a super spiritual, non-gender specific environment that just can't be bothered with romantic interests. However, those are the typical assumptions we make when we interpret Jesus' words. It's interesting that Jesus began his reply with, "You are mistaken, not knowing the Scriptures nor the power of God." I believe the current theories about eternity could be bravely reformed if we just considered the scriptures instead of our assumptions.

What we're doing now is building a foundation for a new theory on eternal romance. We've seen how romance played a part in the first eternal experience, in the garden before the fall of man. And we've seen how the most common scriptural argument regarding future romantic relationships is seriously flawed. But there's one more condition Jesus put on any future male/female relationships. He said we won't be married or given in marriage, and I like to take His words at face value. When Jesus says something so clearly and literally, there is no point in looking for something contradictory. That means if we were to stop right here, we'd have to conclude that there must be some kind of male/female relationship in eternity, but it won't look like marriage as we now know it.

Before we attempt a theory about it, let me make one important disclaimer: When things were perfect, it was one man and one woman in an eternal, holy, and exclusively intimate relationship. If a person veers from this simple foundation, they might come up with all sorts of theories that reflect dark desires more than God's perfect pattern. Historically, this is exactly what has happened. In an attempt to find a "higher" truth, people have destroyed the exclusivity of romance in modern "free love" and casual sex movements. If given the leeway, they might think Heaven reflects these values as well. But I believe that is as great a mistake as assuming eternal life is devoid of romantic passion. In short, eternity is not a hippie, free love experience where everyone is romantic with whomever they choose. And it isn't a gathering of celibate, asexual robots who just want to play worship music on their harps all day long, either. Whatever it is it must be as simple, and as holy, and as beautiful as it was in the beginning.

Chapter 18

One Life

Jesus said that at the resurrection we wouldn't marry or be given in marriage anymore. This effectively put a time limit on the covenant of marriage. It is a temporal covenant that only applies to our mortal experience of life. This is why most marriage vows contain the phrase, "till death do you part." Once we are dead, our experience as a fallen creation is over. We will put off the mortal, corrupted life and put on the incorruptible life of immortality. For all of us in Christ, marriage – as we know it – will be a thing of the past. Since I've suggested that the end of "marriage" does not necessarily mean an end to romance, it remains to be seen what could take its place. Naturally, if we want to know how immortals experience romance, we need to keep looking at the first couple chapters of Genesis. And the first question we need to ask is, "Were Adam and his wife actually married?"

> *"Remember that the Lord could not find anything on the outside of Adam to be a suitable companion for him. Everything that had been made, and even the Godhead, could not fulfill that role. So God took something from within that original person, and thus separated one creation – one life – into two distinct parts."*

To begin, let's establish what marriage is to us today in our temporal, fallen experience. The official definition is a union between a man and woman that is recognized by law. That sounds a little clinical, and we all know there's much more to it than that. For instance, most people discover their attraction to the opposite sex long before they are ever married. Then they spend the intermediate years looking for that future spouse. They meet many different people they might consider as a possible mate, and then, in a moment of decision, they choose one of those persons as a spouse. Even if the choosing is done by the parents or a third party as it is in some cultures, the effect is still the same. It is two completely separate people coming together in a legal and exclusive union.

That brings us to a fundamental difference between the union of Adam and his wife and what we experience in marriage today. Adam and Eve were not two separate people who happened upon each other at the park one day and hit it off. They were two halves of the same, unified person. It's interesting to note that Adam's wife isn't called Eve until after the fall of man. Until then, they both might have been called Adam. Or perhaps Adam-her and Adam-him. Who really knows? The point is that they were not two separate people. They were made from the exact same genetic stock – only they had been split into the male and female components of that original, whole person. Let's think back to the previous chapter: Remember that the Lord could not find anything on the outside of Adam to be a suitable companion for him.

Everything that had been made, and even the Godhead, could not fulfill that role. So God took something from within that original person, and thus separated one creation –

one life – into two distinct parts. The basic difference between their union and what we call marriage is an issue of direction. Adam and Eve found each other from within. Everyone today finds their respective spouses from without. The first couple was the only couple on record to have experienced this kind of union, and I can only surmise this is because they lived before the fall of mankind. Once the perfect reflection was shattered, the perfect union between male and female was shattered along with it.

This subject can get a bit metaphysical and a little hard to grasp. Let's say it one more time so that we really get what's going on here. The first person ever created was a completely unified, whole person. Both the male and female genders were being expressed in Adam. When God wanted to make a companion for Adam, He didn't create a separate person (that would have been finding a companion from without). Instead, God took the female part out of Adam, and then showed him his female counterpart. From that point on, the first person existed as two separate and autonomous persons. But they were forever joined together as man and wife; and their union was, for lack of a better description, the eternal version of marriage. While this may seem hard to understand, keep in mind that we believe the exact same thing about God. Isn't God made up of separate, distinct persons who also exist as a unified, whole life? Do we believe that those parts are both male and female? Do we also believe Adam and his wife were made as a perfect 3-D copy of God? If the answer to all of that is "yes", then we might start to see how much was really lost in the fall of mankind.

I theorize that one cannot exist as just an individual (or single) male or female and be as whole and as perfect as mankind was created to be. In the same way, God cannot be God if any one of the persons – or genders – of the Godhead is missing. In order to be perfect again, it makes sense to me that we must be joined to a perfect counterpart. As I said before, I don't think we will lose our gender, and we are not supposed to express all the genders by ourselves. We need to be just as we are, but perfectly joined to our companion. If this turns out to be the case, then in that union, we will finally look like a perfect 3-D copy of God. It needs to be pointed out that, in this union, I don't think we will lose our sense of self or individuality, either. We only need to look at the persons of the Godhead to see that they are perfectly individual *and* perfectly united.

Now I think we can answer our question. Were Adam and Eve married? No. They did not find each other at a social mixer in the garden one day and then decide to get married. They were two halves of the exact same genetic source, and they were made to be with each other. If they weren't married, were they in some kind of union? Yes! The words "husband" and "wife" are even used to describe their relationship; but, curiously, the word "marriage" is never used. That idea doesn't come into play until the latter parts of Genesis, *after* the fall.

What Adam and Eve had can't accurately be called marriage, because it isn't an external union of totally separate people. But it must be called something. Don't hold your breath, because with the exception of "eternal romance," I'm out of ideas. Just remember that the whole point of this original couple was so that they would have true companionship. Loneliness was the only part of the first creation that God said wasn't good. It wasn't good for Adam to have all the parts wrapped up inside himself, and it wasn't good for God to make another whole person for him to be with. The only perfect solution was to differentiate Adam into separate beings who could enjoy their distinctions and reunions for a blessed eternity.

All of this goes back to Jesus' teaching on romance after the resurrection. Since He said we wouldn't marry anymore, we have to reckon that marriage is not what Adam and Eve participated in, and we have to be open to something greater coming on the horizon. In order to theorize what that will be, I think we have to pay special attention to the other reason the Sadducees were in error. Jesus said they didn't know the power of God. So let's contemplate what will happen at the resurrection, knowing that God is very, very powerful.

Remember to hang in there with me as I continue on in this purely theoretical pursuit of questions and potential answers with respect to all of this! But I believe it's possible that when we are restored to immortality, we will find that our new, incorruptible DNA contains enough information for not one, but two whole people. And then I believe God will do the exact same thing for us that He did with the first person. He will pull that DNA away from us and show it to us as another person, only of the opposite gender.

The perfection of that union is something we can only dream about, but I believe it is worth considering since I believe that we stand at the door of the next age. Now imagine this — an eternal kingdom of perfect genetic counterparts, existing in complete unity and companionship. Each couple experiencing the joys of individuality and reunion in an everyday expression of love in all its forms. If this sounds like a kingdom of Adams and Eves, than maybe we're onto something here. Before we conclude this topic, I'd like to point out some obvious effects of this theory when you consider it. First, I'm a married man, and my wife and I have talked about these things at length. As you can imagine, this can be a delicate subject. For instance, if a look ahead into romance in the next age made my mortal marriage seem less significant, I would worry. Remember, if the fruit of a discovery is bad, that is a major cause for alarm.

Instead, what I found as I pondered marriage and romantic union in immortality was a newfound joy and appreciation of marriage in a fallen state. It is the most amazing act of grace imaginable. When I think of my wife and I existing together, with all of the joys and hardships that come with it, I come away thinking it's a miracle we have been afforded this companionship at all. We are two totally different and corruptible creatures on our way to a total restoration. And yet, in our marriage, we've been given a glimpse of love and union that is irreplaceable. There is simply no way I would even be asking these kinds of questions if not for my wife. It's all of our experiences, all of our conversations, and the joys of being together that have formulated the basic question – if this is so good, what must be coming next? Simply put, knowing that there is something different about romance in eternity has not in any way diminished romance in mortality. It has only reaffirmed it as a holy matrimony.

Aside from marriage, there are other relationships that are safe, provisional, and blessed, even though they are limited to our earthly sojourn. Take for example the relationship between biological parents and children. I do not expect my son and daughter will call me "dad" when we are all immortal, even though I think they will most certainly recognize me as their mortal father. They have a heavenly Father whom I am keen for them to meet. But that does not weaken my role as a father here and now. Rather, it intensifies it. I am going to do the very best job I can to relay the nature and actions of the heavenly Father, so that their relationship with Him develops as effortlessly as possible. As a father, I want them to be prepared for eternity.

In the same way, if we are brave enough to ponder the future of romance, then I think we will see a similar strengthening of our romantic unions right now, even as the day of our immortality approaches. Might we do the very best job we can as earthly spouses, knowing that very soon something even better is on the way? In this manner, can't a husband and wife prepare each other for eternity in the same way parents would their children?

There are endless theories we can have on all of this and we will only know the correct ones when we finally ascend to our heavenly home for good and find out these wonderful mysteries for ourselves. But personally, and for the sake of continuing the discussion I've begun in this chapter, the theory I've presented is one that seems logical and desirable to me, given that I am very happily married here on earth.

If I'm not going to be married to my wife after the resurrection, but I am going to be joined together with a female companion, it makes tons of sense that the companion isn't *another* woman. If that were true can you imagine the awful and awkward encounters that would take place in eternity? Can you imagine running into your mortal spouse, only to see them with some other person who was better fit for them than you were? That seems illogical and downright weird.

I have often thought of that humorous possibility of happening upon my mortal spouse walking in the Garden, only to see her with some other guy who lived thousands of years before her and on some different continent. Then, I imagine getting annoyed and asking, "What was wrong with me? Why is this guy a better fit for her than I was?" You can see why a scenario like this would get confusing (or possibly comical). I think that is what's at the heart of the Sadducee's question. If the woman in their hypothetical situation had been married to all 7 brothers, how in the world is it determined which one is best? And, what is to become of the other 6 brothers not joined to her in eternity? Since they were all intimate with her, how is all of that not really, really awkward?

However, if you were to run into your former spouse and see them walking around the garden with *themselves* (so to speak), I imagine it would leave you with a totally different feeling. You would not find your mortal spouse with a replacement partner who is in any way comparable to you. It is not another person who is somehow better suited to be joined to them. It is simply their perfect, completely restored life being expressed in two separate people. For that is what Adam and Eve really were, individually alive and separate expressions of one life. And of course, that is what God is as well.

There's one more side to this story and to my theoretical musings, and it pertains to all those who want to remain single. Jesus and Paul both spoke about celibacy, and they both implied that it was better not to marry. Neither of them required it of people, but they affirmed those who felt called to it. Paul said it is desirable because the "time is short" (1 Corinthians 7:49). I wonder if both of these men spoke about temporal celibacy because of the eternal romance to come? Certainly, they presented singleness as a way to stay focused on the kingdom of God, but it could have other benefits. If someone has abstained from an earthly marriage, they may be particularly ready to enter into an eternal covenant with their perfect companion. There would be nothing to compare in that case, whether good or bad. Traditionally, though, anyone considering celibacy is told that they are giving up their one chance to experience a romantic relationship.

As I've pointed out, I just don't think that's true. This leads me to mention one more possible effect of this theory: If young people are taught that eternity contains a romance even greater than what we know today, and that abstaining from it is a mortal choice, nothing more, then will more believers choose to do what Jesus and Paul said was "better?" I think so, and I have personally wondered if that would be a sign of the end of the age. If more and more people begin to discover their eternal lives, then I wonder if they are bound to come to similar conclusions about this, even if they don't read this book? It may be that people become so caught up to the eternal realms that they are content to patiently wait for their immortal fulfillment.

Chapter 19

Testing the Theories

Most of the time, we come up with a theory because we observe some phenomenon and then ask ourselves, "How can that be?" We contemplate it to try to understand it, and that process played out for me over and over again during my heavenly journeys. So while I understand that there will be many other types of theories put forward by others' experiences in Heaven, I have to go on my own, personal experiences to be able to articulate and contemplate my own theories, some of which were put into this book.

To give a few instances, when I started reading the book Stars for All Seasons (that book I found in my heavenly library), it lead me to contemplate time and the story of redemption in ways I had never imagined. Then there was an experience in the Spirit when I began hearing a distinctly feminine and nurturing voice talking to me while in that Godly realm. That brought on some speculation about the Holy Spirit's identity. Furthermore, when I finally began to glimpse the Holy Spirit as my heavenly Mother, I had to give those issues even more serious thought. And, as you can guess, when I saw myself in the Spirit, living a perfect, immortal life with a perfect female companion/partner, I had to do some intense theorizing to try and figure that part out. "How can that be?" is a very common sentiment for me in the heavenly realms.

I trusted my experiences, even though they stretched me, and I wrote about how I learned to trust those heavenly journeys in my other books. But even though I believed it, I still had a strong desire to *understand* it, and I always wanted to make sure my experiences were kept on track in light of the scriptures and the overall plan of God. You can look back at the section on discovery to see why we have to test all of our next age ideas to make sure their fruit is holy and life giving.

"I am completely confident that we will get it all sorted out and that the fruit will be good. At the end of the day, God is still in charge of the transition."

You might also recall that I approached many of these issues cautiously, even though I was delighted at what was being revealed. I was very aware that people get excited about their experiences, but later find themselves way off the path, and it could have all been avoided if there was some honest discernment and examination. Asking that basic question, "How can that be?" is a great way to make sure our experiences don't run away with us. If all of this sounds a little risky or vulnerable, then you're getting the right picture, and here again we get into the very nature of a transition between the cosmic ages.

In the transition, our experiences and corresponding theories are still formulating. It's a fragile time, much like the moment a crustacean grows out of its former shell. When it molts the old covering off, a lobster (or something like it) is particularly vulnerable until the new skin hardens into its larger, protective shell. But in order to grow, this fragile state has to be embraced. In other words, to forward the story, we have to go through a time when being vulnerable, like the molting lobster, is an absolute necessity.

If we forget to discern, or forget the history of discovery, or lose track of the principles that got us this far in our journey of restoration, then our vulnerability might be taken advantage of. Despite what I'm about to bring up, I am completely confident that we will get it all sorted out and that the fruit will be good. At the end of the day, God is still in charge of the transition. But I think it's worth noting a few examples of next age efforts that just fell short. Let's take a look at some of these "false starts" to get a better picture of what we must avoid.

The first and most glaring example is the one that capitalized on the concept of a coming age. Of course, we know it as the New Age movement. I'd be wrong to only paint a condemning picture of this effort not only because I should not judge according to the directives of Jesus, but also because there really are some admirable things that came out of it. To begin with, so called New Agers were open to spiritual things at a time when western culture was becoming increasingly materialistic. They believed there was a spiritual component to life that could be explored and interacted with, and that's worth noting. They also popularized a feminine image of God, which is also strangely appropriate given the theories we've covered. But in spite of some forward progress in those areas, the New Age movement regressed in the areas that matter most.

Instead of getting closer to God, New Agers found themselves farther away, simply by forgetting the story of God and Man as told throughout the history of discovery. For 6,000 years, God had been drawing Man back into a close, familial embrace that was more and more personal with each new age. Yet in the New Age movement, God was often reduced to an impersonal, undefined deity. He (or She) was called the supreme force in the universe, or the universe as a conscious whole, or even a slightly more personal take on karma. And Jesus, if He was given any consideration, was often just considered another inspired teacher.

As for their feminine notion of God? That took the form of another kind of deity altogether. Sometimes she was called mother earth, Lilith, or even a goddess of wisdom known as Sophia. Again, the overarching theme was a move towards an impersonal and unknown god or goddess or perhaps the obtainment of some sort of godlike status, themselves. It's as if the entire history of discovery – the entire narrative of the restoration of Man – was set aside for a humanistic, neopagan search for meaning. (What an amazing achievement for the same deceiver who convinced Eve she could have some sort of special knowledge and be "like God" without losing anything!)

> "If an idea about the next age moves us backwards in our relationship with God, then it cannot be the real thing. I'm tempted to regard this quality – the enrichment and the closeness of our relationship with God – as the quality by which all the next age theories should be tested. Ultimately, that quality is an indicator of our restoration. And that has been the whole point of the last 6,000 years of human history."

This is a sad tale, because they were on to something. In my opinion, they were right about the cosmic ages and they were right about the femininity of God (or, rather, a *part* of God), but the overall effect of the New Age movement is a *regression* in the story, and that's the only kind of criticism I'm comfortable giving. If an idea about the next age moves us backwards in our relationship with God, then it cannot be the real thing. I'm tempted to regard this quality – the enrichment and the closeness of our relationship with God – as the quality by which all the next age theories should be tested. Ultimately, that quality is an indicator of our restoration. And that has been the whole point of the last 6,000 years of human history.

Another example can be found in places like the Mormon church, also known as the Latter Day Saint (or LDS) church. They believe that their founder discovered another testament of Jesus Christ, and it didn't bother them at all to add it to the orthodox scriptures. You'd have to be very comfortable with the principle of discovery to do something like that. Also, in their own way, they even tackled the issue of eternal romance with their thoughts on being "sealed" to their earthly spouses. Whether or not we agree with those doctrines (and I don't), I think they show us that "next stage" thinking was at least being attempted in the Mormon church.

But when we look at the fruit of those progressive ideas, we are left with the same conclusion we had with the New Age movement. Instead of going further in the story of our redemption, it takes a step backwards. A quick study of all the regulations Mormons have to follow and the religious rituals they are expected to perform is the best way to see what I'm talking about. There are temple ceremonies, ritual baptisms and washings, dietary restrictions, and even special undergarments. The workload a Mormon has to shoulder to be in God's favor is... well... a little Old Testament, only worse, because this regimented task list comes after the freeing resurrection of Jesus! This is hardly what I would expect from a group claiming to be so progressive – or a group claiming to believe in Jesus. When any religious system relies so heavily on rituals and regulations to gain God's favor, it has become religious in the worst sense of the word. Notice that in the history of discovery, the closer we get to God, the less "religious" we become.

Just to give one more example, listen to the way the LDS church instructs its followers to address God. The ever more *personal* titles like the Hebrew word equivalent to "Daddy" that we see in the New Testament, have been replaced with impersonal, pseudo-holy, titles like "Thee" and "Thou." It may seem like a small issue, but how you address God in prayer is a good indicator of how close the relationship really is. If you have to be formal with Him (and that is what referring to God as "Thee" and "Thou" really is – a formality), then you are not familiar with Him. My kids don't call me Mr. Carter. They call me Dad. Remember, the direction of the history of discovery is towards increasing closeness and familiarity, not the other way around.

"To reiterate, the next age will bring a closer relationship with God, not one that is more distant. It will have to include something even more familial than what Jesus introduced when He told us to pray, "Our Father." By default, it will have to be

another step away from worthless religious actions and towards an actual, effortless identity as a son or daughter of God. Therefore, any movement that claims to be of the next age, but doesn't show the fruit of an even closer relationship with the Lord, must be a deception, or at the very least seriously flawed."

I'm aware the criticisms I've made are big generalizations, and I don't mean them to condemn the individual people involved in these groups. I have friends and family in both the LDS church and New Age movement, and I love and respect them all. The reason I'm bringing these two groups up for discussion (among many more examples I could use) is because they are both trying to reveal the next chapter of the story. In addition to that, they are both unorthodox and certainly on the fringe. That's just what the ideas in this book are, also – believe me, I realize that. It's just "part of the deal" that all efforts to help usher in the next age will probably be categorized together, regardless of their respective validity or actual similarity to one another. So sooner or later, someone is going to make a comparison, and I'd like there to be a standard for judging what is truly of the next age and what falls short.

To reiterate, the next age will bring a closer relationship with God, not one that is more distant. It will have to include something even more familial than what Jesus introduced when He told us to pray, "Our Father." By default, it will have to be another step away from worthless religious actions and towards an actual, effortless identity as a son or daughter of God. Therefore, any movement that claims to be of the next age, but doesn't show the fruit of an even closer relationship with the Lord, must be a deception, or at the very least seriously flawed.

However, if we do find a theory that passes the test, then it just might be something that can help prepare us for life in the next age. That's ultimately the job of any transitionary – to help close the door on the old paradigm and prepare the way for a brand new season of growth.

Finis

Lightning Source UK Ltd.
Milton Keynes UK
UKHW012029191020
371846UK00001B/259